W9-DGJ-989

logolounge 6

2,000 International Identities by Leading Designers

BEVERLY MASSACHUSETTS

ROCKPORT PUBLISHERS

Catharine Fishel and Bill Gardner

© 2011 by Bill Gardner
Paperback edition published 2012
All rights reserved. No part of this book may be reproduced in any form without written permission of the copyright owners. All images in this book have been reproduced with the knowledge and prior consent of the artists concerned, and no responsibility is accepted by producer, publisher, or printer for any infringement of copyright or otherwise, arising from the contents of this publication. Every effort has been made to ensure that credits accurately comply with information supplied. We apologize for any inaccuracies that may have occurred and will resolve inaccurate or missing information in a subsequent reprinting of the book.

First published in the United States of America by

Rockport Publishers, a member of

Quayside Publishing Group

100 Cummings Center

Suite 406-L

Beverly, Massachusetts 01915-6101

Telephone: (978) 282-9590

Fax: (978) 283-2742

www.rockpub.com

Library of Congress Control Number: 2010933488

ISBN: 978-1-59253-824-9

10 9 8 7 6 5 4 3 2 1

DC Comic images © DC Comics, All rights reserved.

Design: Gardner Design

Layout & Production: *tabula rasa* graphic design

Production Coordinator: Lauren Kaiser / Gardner Design

Cover Image: Gardner Design

Printed in China

To Crew 318, Denny, Alex, Andrew, Sam, and Bill: thank you.

—Catharine Fishel

A decimal dedication with much to be thankful for:
Millions of hits on LogoLounge.com annually;
Hundred thousand-plus logos uploaded to this site;
Ten thousand-plus memebers of LogoLounge.com;
One thousand-plus designers included in this book;
One Hundred-plus countries our members call home;
Ten Gardner Design and LogoLounge.com partners;
One daughter and one wife who make my life pure joy.

—Bill Gardner

contents

introduction

I think the craft of logo design is as close to brain surgery as designers ever come. If there is an aspect of design that tests the complete skill set and the foundation of knowledge for the designer, this is it. Brevity is the soul of a great logo. Anyone can ultimately define a concept if they are given an unlimited number of words with which to do so. Carving out a succinct solution in three strokes of the pen is a different feat altogether.

Think about the value any entity must place on their logo. Imagine the lifting this icon is responsible for. Yet if it is successful, it must convey a wealth of emotion and information in the blink of an eye. It is true that a mark becomes imbued with greater meaning over a period of time, but only if the designer can engage the audience. I believe great identity designers have developed an innate ability to sense when a mark is perfected. Something in your heart tells you an image is right. You know when there is 5 percent too little detail or 15 percent too much. You can tell if a concept is buried too deep or when it waits appropriately just beneath the surface, ready to unveil itself in an ah-ha moment

How a designer reaches that level of expertise is a unique path for each. I recall illustrator Tim Biskup sharing a story that a mentor in his early career told him: "Every artist has 10,000 bad drawings inside of them; the secret is to get them out early so you can move on to the good ones." It's a sly way of suggesting that no one reaches perfection without a tremendous amount of practice. This is equally true with logo design; there is a corollary here. Great identity designers have taken the time to mentally dissect thousands of logos to understand why they are exceptional and how they work.

The 2,000 highly organized logos in this book were selected from more than 35,000 submissions made since the last selection process for *LogoLounge 5*. This is a monumental collection, and it attests to the stamina of the panel of eight astonishingly talented judges who were faced with the daunting task of selecting only the very best.

Members of LogoLounge.com can see all of this work—in fact, you may view every logo submitted to past, present, or future books by joining LogoLounge.com. Additionally, members receive unlimited uploads of their own logos for possible inclusion in future books. At the time of this writing, LogoLounge has a database of nearly 135,000 logos, contributed by members from more than 100 countries around the world. Each of these logos is searchable by keyword, industry, designer, date, client, and style.

This book is more than a showcase for the most exceptional logos of our times. It is also an opportunity for designers to discover how common and how diverse the identity design process is across the globe. Dozens of logo case studies create a chance for the reader to empathize with others in their design trials and the opportunity to stand on their shoulders from the lessons learned.

Travel through the backstory and the boardroom as designers weave through challenging obstacles to create visual identities for the likes of television networks, art galleries, banks, retail stores, and restaurants. Note the diversity of approaches as these projects are tackled by the largest multinational brand firms and the smallest design studios. Experience the process through the eyes of world's leading typographic designers and also through the minds of today's most celebrated conceptual design theorists. From the purist to the renegade designer, these stories will provide you with incredible insight and tools you will welcome and embrace.

Among the exceptional logos organized in this book, there are sure to be a few one-hit wonders. At the same time, you may be confident that many of the works are from certifiable masters of the craft. However, one of the most amazing aspects of any LogoLounge book is the guarantee that somewhere in these pages, whether it's evident yet or not, resides the early work of the next generation of identity geniuses.

—Bill Gardner

jurors

Hans Hulsbosch
Hulsbosch Strategy & Design, Sydney, Australia

Killed Productions, by Sean Heisler

"The best logos are always the ultra-simple ones because they will be remembered, and this one surely will be. I first saw it late last year on the LogoLounge website, and I remember thinking, the designer could have used a gun, bullet holes, blood, the usual. But instead he used typography, and the impact is far better. Also, it doesn't apply to any trend; it is timeless. Simplicity is key, so no wonder it is my favorite."

Hans Hulsbosch was born in the Netherlands. He studied and worked in Amsterdam during the 1970s, before moving to Sydney, Australia, in 1979. He worked as the creative director of the top advertising agency until 1985 and opened his own strategy and design company. He

has designed many of Australia's iconic brands, such as Qantas (he was part of the team who redesigned the Qantas "flying kangaroo" in 1985 and he designed the latest version in 2007), Woolworths supermarkets, P&O Cruises, the MLC "nest egg," and Taronga Zoo, to name a few. His company has also designed many of Australia's leading packaging brands.

Sherwin Schwartzrock
Schwartzrock Graphic Arts, Minnetonka, Minnesota

Ponzu Sushi House, by Keo Pierron

"As a designer who is also an artist, I'm always attracted to beautifully rendered marks that are more artistic than practical . . . of which there are lots in this book. However, when I take off the artist hat and think strategically as a graphic designer, for me the perfect logo is one that (1) states the name of the company, (2) conveys what they sell, (3) captures the spirit of the company, and (4) does all of these visual things quickly and efficiently. The logo for Ponzu meets all of these requirements. Sure, it doesn't have as much artistic pizzazz as other marks in this book, but I guarantee you, this logo will work hard and efficiently for its owner."

At the age of thirteen, Sherwin Schwartzrock began drawing a weekly comic strip for a dozen Minnesota newspapers and freelanced as an illustrator throughout high school. After graduating, he found work at

a local ad agency while attending Minnesota State University–Moorhead, studying under Professor Phil Mousseau. Minneapolis design pioneer John Reger asked Sherwin to joined Design Center after college, where he rose to vice president at age twenty-seven. In 2001, he started Schwartzrock Graphic Arts and now collaborates closely with 3,2,1, a brand-strengthening firm that informs the visual solutions his company provides for a wide range of clients.

Silvio Giorgi
Latinbrand, Quito, Ecuador

Tetris, by Britt Funderburk
"I like when a logotype tells a story. The Tetris logotype made me smile and reminds me of the long hours that I spend playing the famous game. This logo has the elements that it needs, it doesn't need color, and it is fun and clever. Great concept."

Originally from Colombia, Silvio Giorgi and his brother, Sandro, founded their own studio in the mid-1990s in Quito, Ecuador. With a multidisciplinary process, they develop corporate identities, packaging, brand documentation, and implementation. In the past sixteen years, Latinbrand has captured and expressed the spirit, personality, and culture of its Latin American clients.

Their portfolio of brands gained attention in the design community, and after a couple of years of fruitful collaboration, they started to receive invitations for countless features in international books and magazines. Their work has been recognized nationally and internationally, and has been featured in the *Graphis Poster and Logo Annual, World Graphics Design, Communications Arts, Latin American & Caribbean Graphic Design Book, Logo Design 2,* and *Brand Identity Now!* With a string of awards for their brands, the multidisciplinary group continues to produce high-quality work for corporate identity and visual communication projects.

TETRIS

Bart Crosby
Crosby Associates, Chicago, Illinois

Vino with Veterans, by Schwartzrock Graphic Arts
"After two days of viewing more than 5,000 logos, my thoughts were: 'haven't I seen this somewhere before?' and 'having an idea is way better than having a computer.'

I purposefully went back to select my favorite more than a week after I'd finished judging—after all, a logo should be memorable and should make a lasting impression. And it should be unique to the client or the initiative or the event for which it was created. And while there were twenty or so that I thought were really outstanding, the one that stuck was AIGA Minnesota's 'Vino with Veterans.' "

Bart Crosby is president of Crosby Associates Inc., Chicago-based specialists in the planning and design of organizational, product, event, and initiative identification and branding programs. Founded in 1979, the company has a client roster that includes multinational corporations, educational institutions, professional associations, financial services firms, government agencies, and individual entrepreneurs.

In addition to managing the firm and relationships with clients, Bart provides strategic and design direction to the firm's projects and programs. His work has been recognized by nearly every professional design organization, and he's been featured in many national and international design and business publications.

jurors

Jessica Hische
Jessica Hische, New York, New York

Snooty Peacock, by Ryan Russell Design
"In order for a logo to be considered 'great' in my eyes, not only does it have to be very well executed, it also has to be smart. Of the thousands of logos submitted to LogoLounge, this logo stood out to me because not only was it executed perfectly, it is such a smart visual representation of the company name. Many logos were beautiful and perfectly executed, but few were as memorable as this mark. It put a smile on my face when I first saw it, and throughout the judging process I couldn't get it out of my head."

Jessica Hische is a typographer and illustrator working in Brooklyn, New York. After graduating from Tyler School of Art with a degree in graphic design, she worked for Headcase Design in Philadelphia before taking a position as senior designer at Louise Fili Ltd. While working for Louise, she continued developing her freelance career, working for clients such as Tiffany & Co., Chronicle Books, and the New York Times. In September 2009, after two and a half years of little sleep and a lot of hand-lettering, she left to pursue her freelance career further. Jessica has been featured in most major design and illustration publications, including *Communication Arts, Print Magazine, How Magazine, The Graphis Design Annual, American Illustration,* and the *Society of Illustrators*. She was featured as one of *Step Magazine*'s 25 Emerging Artists, *Print Magazine*'s New Visual Artists 2009 (commonly referred to as "Print's 20 under 30"), and The Art Directors Club Young Guns. She was named Lettercult's Person of the Year 2009. She has released one typeface, called Buttermilk, which is available at both www.myfonts.com and www.veer .com, and is best known for her ongoing project, Daily Drop Cap, in which she illustrates a decorative letter every day.

Marius Ursache
Grapefruit, Iasi, Romania

AIGA Minnesota, by Schwartzrock Graphic Arts
"I know nothing about Minnesota. But the combination is simple and smart, and would definitely make me want to join AIGA."

Marius should have been a successful plastic surgeon (he holds a medical degree from the University of Medicine and Pharmacy in Romania), but as a young student he landed a part-time job in media and advertising. After working as a cartoonist and graphic artist for a radio station and then for a national media trust, he went on to be a designer and art director for agencies in the United Kingdom and the United States. Then, in 1999, he founded Grapefruit, one of the first branding agencies in Romania.

Meanwhile, he started studying design in New York at Sessions College, and then with Milton Glaser at the School of Visual Arts. He continued with a master's degree at SNSPA Bucharest and now is studying digital communication in a European Master of Interactive Multimedia program. He holds an impressive pile of international prizes, among which the most recent is a Brand Leadership Award from World Brand Congress 2009 in India.

Tessa Westermeyer
Landor, Geneva, Switzerland

Jugar Creative, by Hernandez Design Studio
"There is a level of simplicity that makes this so compelling; the use of positive and negative creates an impactful result. It is so successful in black and white, however, that I could imagine it executed in a range of very graphic primary colors. There is timelessness in this design. It harkens back to a simpler era, although it still has a fresh and relevant feel today."

Tessa has more than twenty-three years of experience in print, package design, corporate identity, and environmental branding. She is energized by the challenge of working across many disciplines, creating strategic solutions that communicate the total brand experience. Tessa has led creative teams in the development of strategic design solutions for a wide range of national and global clients, including Procter & Gamble, Disney, Marriott Hotels, Timberland, Starbucks, Coca-Cola, Key Bank, Barnes and Noble Books and Music, Sony Canada, and Jockey.

She now lives in Geneva, where she leads a creative team for the Landor Geneva regional office.

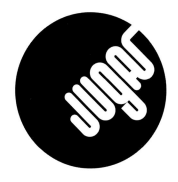

Jeannie Servaas
Wolff Olins, New York, New York

EVCI, by bartodell.com
"I'm usually a freak about hand-drawn, illustrative logos, so I thought I'd give a shout out to modern, clever, and simple elegance this time."

Jeannie currently works as a design director at Wolff Olins, a branding firm in New York. She graduated from the Yale School of Art with a master's degree in graphic design in 2003. Since then, she has developed and presented concepts for projects involving a broad range of media. Jeannie's approach is based on her experience bridging the worlds of art and design to bring a unique vision to the clients she works with. Prior to joining Wolff Olins, her seven-year design career included work for clients such as Nokia, Herman Miller, Amdocs, Apollo Tyres, Swiss Re, Ford, Virgin, Nike, MTV, Sundance, VH1, TBS, VIVA Plus, the USA Channel, and RES Magazine.

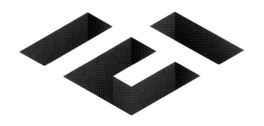

portraits

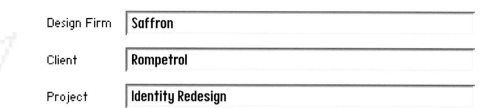

Design Firm	Saffron
Client	Rompetrol
Project	Identity Redesign

Consider the standard gas/petrol station with requisite convenience store. It presents a relatively utilitarian picture, no more than a stop for vehicles and their drivers to refuel. The lights are harsh, the branding messages—from the station and from the hundreds of other brands it sells—strident and abrupt.

As a rule, none of this is offensive because this is what we've come to expect from this retail category. But it's also what makes the new Litro brand, created by Saffron, so remarkable.

Rompetrol is the second largest private petrol company in Romania, with an extensive network in Eastern Europe. It is a very ambitious company,

> The idea was to be the practical gas station, very uncomplicated and straightforward, providing a completely new experience for drivers.

with budget for expansion into areas of Western Europe. Saffron worked with Rompetrol to rebrand and renovate stations in Romania, and, although these projects were successful, the company's expansion into Europe presented new roadblocks.

The Romanian brand was not well accepted there. Romanian goods, in general, did not have a stellar reputation, nor were they especially well known. In fact, a new network in southeast France was not at all successful.

It was clear that a completely new brand, one that could thrive alongside existing European brands such as BP and Repsol, was needed. The Saffron design team could imagine how the new brand could even outshine these brands, literally and financially.

"We wanted to create something from scratch," explains Jacob Benbunan, CEO and founder of Saffron. "The idea was to be the practical gas station, very uncomplicated and straightforward, providing a completely new experience for drivers."

The new brand also needed to instill pride in investors and employees. Local governments, too, needed to be impressed. "When a long stretch of highway is developed," explains Benbunan, "it is these bodies who decide which stations to place where. Rompetrol wanted to make sure its stations were attractive and different enough to be desirable."

LITRO

Litro has a very different sort of identity for a petrol station. Its logo's droplet design suggests refreshment—through fuel or nourishment—but its glowing, simple nature feeds the entire brand experience.

Saffron designers wanted to create a very different sort of brand experience for Litro customers. Unlike other stations where visitors are bombarded with messaging, stopping at Litro was meant to be a calming, quiet, and very comprehensible event. These visuals show a variety of directions, early in the project.

But what could be different about a gas station? It would sell fuel and food. But what if the design of the station itself was modular so that other features, such as a laundromat, could be added? What if the fueling experience could be improved? What if the entire experience could be improved?

Saffron's team began by revamping the name of the station chain. A very simple name was needed, something that was memorable and clear from a vehicle zipping past.

The result was a mix of the unit of measurement by which fuel is sold—the liter—and the international code for Romania—RO. Combining the two to form "Litro" couldn't have been simpler. In addition, it's a very unique name that differentiates it from corporate-sounding competitors.

The visual expression of the name was more complicated. Other station brands, such as BP, are actually very progressive and have decent logos and graphic systems. So, just having a memorable logo would not be enough.

"When you think of BP and Shell, they have great, long histories, but as typical petrol stations, they are very monolithic and static. They don't involve the consumer at all," says Mila Linares, consultant at Saffron. "We wanted to create a dynamic brand that would involve consumers in a more

emotive way through light and sound—allow them to really experience what Litro is all about."

The design team worked on very different logo concepts. From the beginning, all concepts focused on building a differentiating, strong graphic language based on a distinctive expression that could complement and interact with the architecture on one hand and, on the other hand, build a strong language for the communication.

Some of the ideas were based on a pictorial approach with a handwritten wordmark; others on a simple logotype and a minimalist, geometric graphic style to mark the station's functions and architecture. There were also ideas around using the "L" shape as the shortcut of the liter measurement or working with big icons to act as beacons on station canopies.

One idea that stood out was that of a droplet. It had a very recognizable shape and could represent fuel, a soft drink, coffee, or a refreshing pause of any sort. It could be portrayed in any color, wrapped with a pattern, made three-dimensional, or lit from within. The droplet was a very straightforward, sophisticated, and memorable shape, but, above all, it challenged the status quo of Petrol brand logos. Its versatility made for a very robust and simple icon that, independent of its color or pattern, could stand for Litro.

The wordmark is based on the Frutiger Next typeface, a simple, functional, yet elegant typeface to complement, rather than compete with, the droplet symbol. At the same time, the chosen typeface is strong enough to work on the signage elements of the stations. Frutiger Next is also the corporate typeface for communication. Although already a classic, the new and improved Frutiger Next is available in a large range of weights and language versions, crucial for Litro's expansion into markets where the Cyrillic alphabet is used.

The station is the most important touch point of the brand. In order to create a new experience that was much different from the monolithic image of the competitors, Saffron defined a color scheme that consists of four different colors plus a gray version. The different color versions are applied randomly within the station environment.

One very extraordinary feature of the new stations is almost ethereal. Every two, five, or ten minutes, depending on the station manager's preference, the lighting in the station area changes color. The color may change from blue to pink, purple, green, or white in the time it takes to fill up the tank. "Since winter nights can be long in that part of the world, the changing colors are a welcome sight," says Gabor Schreier, creative director at Saffron. "On very long highways, the stations may be set to change more frequently, maybe every two minutes, catching the drivers' attention and helping them identify the stores from a great distance."

The architecture of the stations embraces the new identity and brings it to life. In addition to very modern typography in the signage, the actual structures, gas pumps, lights, and other features are very clean. Saffron teamed up with Eight, Inc., to create the stations.

"There is a real sense of purpose in the design," says Schreier. "Any driver approaching and then using the station would know exactly where to fuel up, pay, or do anything else. Gone are the complicated and competing messages found at other stations. Compared to them, Litro is almost peaceful."

The first two Litro stations were built in the summer of 2009 on the highway that connects Bucharest to Constanta on the Black Sea, with six to eight more planned.

Implementation of the brand in the actual environment proved out the philosophy behind the design. All elements are simple and clean.

One of the key elements of the new Litro design is light. Periodically, the light color of an entire Litro station changes. It's an effect that can be seen from a long distance, and its warm quality serves as a welcoming beacon during long, cold winters.

More views of the new Litro identity in motion

Apollo
Identity Redesign

Saffron, London, England

Apollo is the leading tire brand in India, but it was not well known in the Western world, more specifically in competitive European markets such as Germany and the United Kingdom, where the company wanted to enter the market with a wide range of world-class passenger vehicle tires for cars and SUVs.

Saffron understood Apollo's problem. Although Apollo is a very good brand of tires, when people think of tires they aren't likely to think of a brand from India. Saffron's goal was to help Apollo reposition itself. In the German market, the new brand was formally introduced at the IZB technology show organized by VW in Wolfsburg in October 2008. It was important to make people understand that if Apollo could engineer tires for some of the most unpredictable roads in the world, it could certainly build tires for the Autobahn.

Saffron was asked by Apollo to create a completely renewed brand for Apollo, one that did not look like a typical tire/automotive product at all. Instead, the client wanted to convey the bold, dynamic, confident, and colorful ethos of India and make a definite statement about this new kid on the block. The company's competition included Michelin, Continental, Bridgestone, Dunlop, Hankook, and Goodyear, but Apollo did not want to adopt a "me too" attitude.

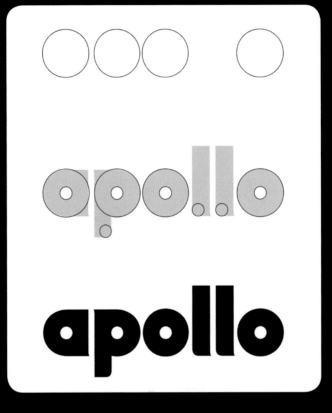

Saffron designers wholeheartedly embraced the bold challenge. They created an identity graphically founded in the symbolism behind the Greek sun god, Apollo. The new system is built around a circle/sun/tire shape, printed in clean, bright colors. The centers of the circles can be made larger or smaller. Repeated in a grid, the pattern almost seems to move or pulse.

But the individual pieces of the pattern weren't purely decorative. Instead, each circle, with its varying center fills and colors, represents a different tire use and variety. The purple inner color stands for radial tires while the orange stands for cross-ply/bias tires. Also, the purple denotes "premium" while the orange signifies "warmth" in the way the company interacts with all stakeholders. The system was built to help the customer dispense with the typically confusing jargon encountered as he or she shopped.

The wordmark for the new design is also based entirely on circles. Letters are built from circles, and they also contain more circles. The circles obviously stand for the sun, the wheel, and mobility. The look is young, bold, and certainly eye-catching—or, as Apollo states, "young, ambitious, Indian, and proud of it."

Above: The new Apollo logo and identity system is based on circles or tires.

The circle theme can be played out in patterning that is eye-catching, whether large or small.

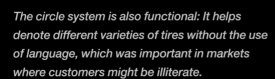

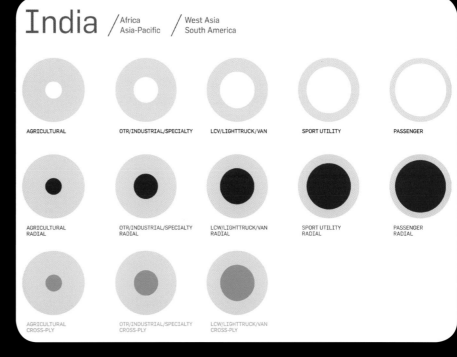

India / Africa / West Asia
Asia-Pacific / South America

AGRICULTURAL	OTR/INDUSTRIAL/SPECIALTY	LCV/LIGHTTRUCK/VAN	SPORT UTILITY	PASSENGER
AGRICULTURAL RADIAL	OTR/INDUSTRIAL/SPECIALTY RADIAL	LCW/LIGHTTRUCK/VAN RADIAL	SPORT UTILITY RADIAL	PASSENGER RADIAL
AGRICULTURAL CROSS-PLY	OTR/INDUSTRIAL/SPECIALTY CROSS-PLY	LCW/LIGHTTRUCK/VAN CROSS-PLY		

The circle system is also functional: It helps denote different varieties of tires without the use of language, which was important in markets where customers might be illiterate.

Design Firm	**Sagmeister**
Client	**Casa da Música**
Project	**Identity Redesign**

When Stefan Sagmeister presented his identity solution to client Casa da Música, a remarkable arts and music space in Porto, Portugal, an equally remarkable group of Porto citizens—800 in number—came to watch and learn. The presentation had been moved twice to accommodate the burgeoning audience, and if the Casa's 1,300-seat hall had been available, it likely would have been filled, so great was the interest in the project.

The larger hall was not available because it was hosting an international piano virtuoso that evening, just part of another full day of culture at Casa da Música: an art exhibition opening at 10 a.m., a sound installation at noon, a large group of disabled children visiting at 1 p.m., followed by Sagmeister's presentation/event at 4 p.m., the virtuoso at 7 p.m., and a rave for some 2,000 people at midnight. Sagmeister attended every single event.

> I thought they should not have a tagline at all.
> If you have to say what you are, you are not it.

Porto is a city in love with the arts. After opening in 2005, Casa da Música quickly became a landmark, a destination, and a hub of civic pride. Citizen interest in and participation with Casa runs high.

"If we had redesigned the logo for Lincoln Center, you would not read about it in the *New York Times*," Sagmeister says. "In Porto, the identity design process had been featured in full-page articles in the general press. The facility is really a manifestation of how well a center can be run through government funding and private donations. The center can host super-popular events as well as esoteric events, and has funds for both. The client was incredibly smart and lovely, and the city and architecture are first-rate."

When Sagmeister's office was brought into the project in 2007, the venue did have an existing logo, simply a literal representation of the building that showed its unusual architecture. The client was also using the tagline, "One house, many musics."

Initially, the client desired to keep the old tagline in the new identity, but Sagmeister did not agree. "I thought they should not have a tagline at all. If you have to say what you are, you are not it. I almost instinctively do not believe in taglines at all. Instead, we made the main trajectory for the project to be how to display the tagline in a visual system without having to say it," he recalls.

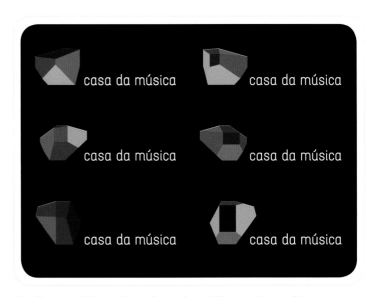

The Casa da Música logo, based on different views of the venue, created by Sagmeister, Inc.

The architecture of the Casa da Música in Porto, Portugal, is extraordinary from any view. The building and the events that it houses are a source of great civic pride for the city. Its new identity, created by Sagmeister, Inc., is as accommodating and as expressive as the place itself.

TOP

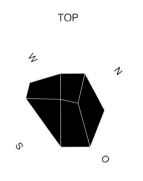

SOUTH VIEW

EAST VIEW

Although initially Stefan Sag-meister did not want to use the shape of the building in the new identity—such identities say more about the architec-ture than what the organiza-tion is about—he eventually came to see the shape as so emblematic of the organization and so representative of the layers' meaning that his team did use the shape. Here, the building is broken into indi-vidual planes.

BOTTOM

NORTH VIEW

WEST VIEW

Another thing the designer did not wish to do was to participate in the pitch for which his office was originally contacted. Three different design compa-nies had been asked to present their ideas. The project especially appealed to Sagmeister's team, which has always been very close to music, person-ally and through design for clients. As music packaging and video projects have gone away as a result of downloads and online presence replacing CDs and other media, their involvement has changed.

"The physical manifestation of music in life has become more and more important, and this project was a great opportunity to design in that space," Sagmeister says.

So, he worked hard to talk the client out of the pitch approach, in the end convincing them to allow his office to handle the project.

Having landed the project, the first thing Sagmeister told the client was that any solution he presented would not involve the architecture of the building. He noted that many identities for such cultural facilities do rely on the architecture to suggest visual cues, but all these really say is that the institution is housed in a beautiful or otherwise remarkable building. The approach does not communicate that this is a music center or that it is a community resource or that it supports many different sorts of music. In this instance, just relying on the shape of the building especially did not say, "one house, many musics."

The client agreed. So, Sagmeister embarked on a two-day visit of Porto to learn what the city and its people were like. He interviewed everyone from the marketing director of Casa da Música to its music director, members of music groups, and participants in community groups. He studied how the building had become an iconic shape in the city and what it meant to its people.

"Koolhaas talks about the building being an exploration of various layers of meaning. I translated his architectural words to words we would use: What are the layers of meaning? Discovering that is what logo making is. If you explore the various layers, you eventually reduce them down to a logo," the designer says. "At that point, we began to understand that the entire building was a logo."

With this new trajectory in mind, the design team assembled six different views of the building—from the east, west, north, south, top, and bottom—and considered the shapes. Which represented the meaning of the building best? It was soon clear that one representation would not convey enough meaning, of the building or of what it contained. Instead, all angles could be used, in addition to interior shapes revealed in transparent views. The building's many asymmetric facets held myriad possibilities.

There were so many possibilities, in fact, that the design team had software written that would actually generate logo directions. Color direction was provided by, say, a photo of an artist who would be performing at Casa da Música or by a painting that might be on display. The software samples fifteen points in the photo or painting and builds a coordinating palette that is applied to surfaces of the logo.

"In a matter of seconds, you have an animated logo that is built from the visual information of the event and from the building stills, all in Photoshop and ready to place," Sagmeister explains. "You still have to select one, but conceptually and through color, the logos will always fit visually. The client can never end up with jarring colors or such."

The chameleon effect works just as well for logo portraits based on photos of Casa da Música employees that are applied to their business cards, or for identities of the various music organizations that the center supports.

"Whether it is for the symphony orchestra or contemporary music, the system works," he adds.

orquestra barocca
casa da música

orquestra barocca
casa da música

orquestra barocca
casa da música

orquestra barocca
casa da música

orquestra barocca
casa da música

orquestra barocca
casa da música

The generated samples can have solid color, textured, or even transparent surfaces.

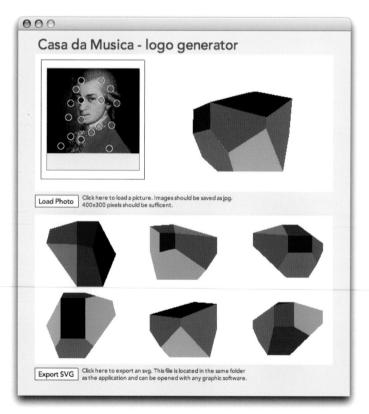

Casa da Musica - logo generator

Load Photo Click here to load a picture. Images should be saved as jpg. 400x300 pixels should be sufficent.

Export SVG Click here to export an svg. This file is located in the same folder as the application and can be opened with any graphic software.

Because the identity had to be so chameleon-like in nature, and to guarantee the client's eventual success with the new identity, the design team created a software program that samples fifteen points on an image and assigns color and/or texture to various forms of the building/logo. "In a matter of seconds, you have an animated logo that is built from the visual information of the event and from the building stills, all in Photoshop and ready to place," Sagmeister explains.

As the city of Porto provides plenty of space for posting promotional posters, the design team suggested that for the first six to seven months of the identity's life the client rely heavily on posters to introduce the new look to the public. These posters would only use the building-shaped logos and color cues from the events as visuals.

After this initial period, the designers and the client began to expand the ways in which the logo shapes could be used—incorporated into photos, for instance, or as part of a larger illustration.

Over time, and now that the client has an in-house design group, the identity based on shapes has continued to grow and develop. Some logos are multicolored, almost jewel-like in their appearance. Others are opaque, like chunks of dense stone, or like line drawings or even ice.

Even though he had initially sworn that the building shape would not drive the design of the logo, Sagmeister says that in this case, even though the architectural shape plays such an enormous part of the overall identity, the end result is still about the content of the building: one house, many musics.

Art direction: Stefan Sagmeister
Design: Matthias Ernstberger, Quentin Walesh
Logo generator: Ralph Ammer

The new graphic can be used as line art, as an object, as part of a photo, as part of an illustration, or even as art itself. These samples are all posters, which were especially effective in Porto, which has plenty of public space for posting.

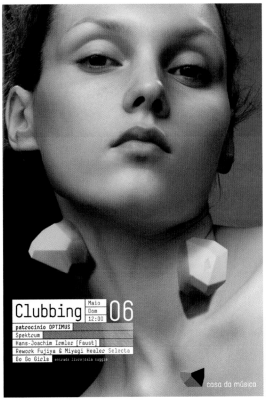

Seed Media
Identity Redesign

Sagmeister, New York, New York

Above: Stefan Sagmeister's identity for Seed Media uses a converted phyllotaxis structure, changing it into a window of pixels that allows colors or images to show through, depending on the subject/event it is representing.

After attending a TED (Technology, Entertainment, Design) Conference, Stefan Sagmeister came away with two related insights: First, he witnessed that complex scientific information could be presented in an exciting and clear manner. The speakers made that abundantly clear.

That first insight revealed another: As a general rule in everyday life, scientific ideas and concepts are not well presented to the layperson. Because media did not share the information well, understanding of and enthusiasm for important scientific issues is often lacking.

These communication problems are something that Seed Media Group, a scientific media company, works hard to solve. Seed Media has been successful in making science sexy and personally meaningful to the general consumer.

Sagmeister took a literal interpretation of Seed Media's goals in creating a new identity for the company. His solution is able to represent all scientific fields, existing and yet to be discovered: He

uses a phyllotaxis structure, a Fibonacci-derived algorithm pattern that is present in many natural aspects of the world, including the seeds in the face of a sunflower, the spiraling leavings on a plant stem, pinecone petals, seashells, pineapples, and the horns of the gazelle, to name a very few, as a literal lens or window through which any science can be viewed.

The designer first converted the basic phyllotaxis structure into a window of pixels. Any image can be viewed through the window, be it a microbe or the head shot of a scientist. Any image is enormously simplified, made more graphic by the extreme reduction of visual information. So, the effect is both literal and highly abstract.

For the client's letterhead, Sagmeister added another twist: He printed the pixilated phyllotaxis with iridescent ink. The ink reflects the surroundings of the setting in which the reader is placed.

Seed Media loved the concept. "The identity was done simply and with love and care," says Sagmeister. This idea was a good match to Seed Media's abilities.

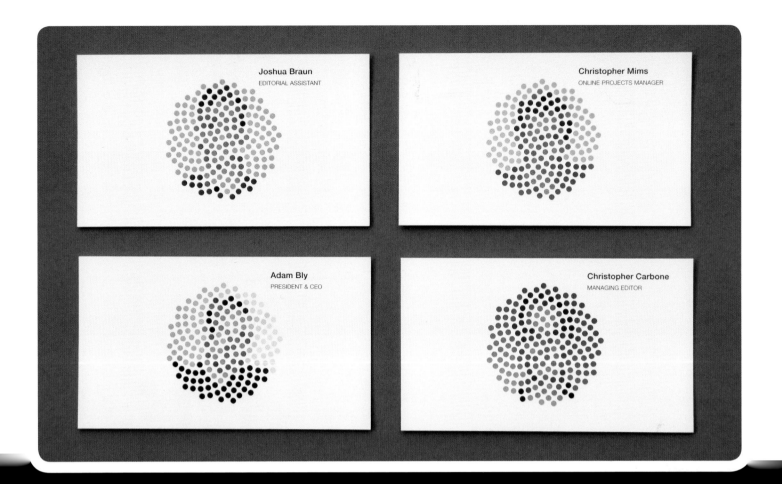

Seed Media employees can also be represented by the phyllotaxis pattern. Each portrait is unique.

Printed in reflective ink, the logo reflects the surroundings of the viewer.

Design Firm	**Office**
Client	**Ogilvy & Mather/IBM**
Project	**Branding Campaign**

"The year 2008 was one of the most volatile years in history, from the meltdown of our financial system, to the ongoing consequences of a global energy crisis, to a health care system teetering on the brink of collapse," says Greg Ketchum, executive creative director for Ogilvy & Mather (New York), IBM's advertising agency. In this extremely challenging marketing landscape, many companies chose to retreat. "IBM saw it as an opportunity to provide new leadership where leadership was urgently needed."

Using its global reach and influence, IBM decided to address the world's biggest problems through its unprecedented Smarter Planet campaign.

> It isn't about marketing products, it's about educating the world that the technology and thinking needed to make the world work better exists today.

"It isn't about marketing products," explains Tom Godici, executive creative director for Ogilvy & Mather (New York). "It's about educating the world that the technology and thinking needed to make the world work better exists today."

With this in mind, IBM's Smarter Planet plan began to take shape in late 2008.

Ogilvy had developed the original globe icon internally, and Godici asked Office (San Francisco) to build on it by developing a visual vocabulary for the campaign.

This involved illustrating a series of lengthy, provocative essays about making the systems of the world smarter, in areas such as energy, traffic, food, banking, and health care.

"Our challenge was to create a graphic language that illustrated these complicated concepts in simple, engaging ways," says Jason Schulte, founder and creative director of Office (San Francisco). The ads included significantly more content than typical print ads, so the accompanying illustrations had to be visually arresting, to draw people in and encourage them to read.

Office was asked by Ogilvy & Mather on behalf of its client IBM to create a visual vocabulary for the Smarter Planet campaign, which began with a series of lengthy, provocative essays about making the systems of the world smarter in areas such as energy, traffic, food, banking, and health care. The result was a series of twenty-one smart, simple icons.

The full suite of IBM Smarter Planet icons. Although the content of each is very different, it's clear that they all are part of a greater effort but that each is a separate and cogent point.

These process boards show many of the icons/illustrations in development. The familial shape, color, and basic personality of the icons are evident.

Billboards from the Smarter Planet campaign. The original globe icon that spawned the entire direction is at far right.

The icons in airport mode.

As the Office team began its work, the designers studied Paul Rand's original creative vision for IBM, which they found was still relevant today.

Rand, whose work for IBM spanned several decades, believed that the company's visual representation should not be based on a strict set of rules and instead should be defined by an attitude and an aspiration, explains Schulte.

"Rand was about boldness and clarity," he says. "And his work usually included a 'wink'-something unexpected that made his work emotionally connect with people." That became a driving force in Office's work.

Office worked with Ogilvy to develop a set of design principles to help create a cohesive vocabulary, so that people recognized the ads as part of a single campaign. This included the thought rays above each icon, the round shape, a consistent color palette (including IBM blue), and the bold, simple illustration style.

"We avoided technology cues and clichés," says Schulte. "We wanted them to be less expected." Each icon has the specificity of an infographic, the visual strength of a successful logo, and the emotional appeal of an illustration.

A new ad ran each week, so the timeline for creating each icon was tight. Schulte calls the process "creative wind sprints."

Once Ogilvy briefed the team with a white paper explaining the essay, Office had two to three days to explore the concept. "There was no time to overthink or overtweak any one sketch—you just had to go," says Schulte. "We started with a very broad range of explorations, sometimes up to 30 per topic, threw them up on boards for our team to discuss, and narrowed down the concepts, making sure they were bold and simple enough to fit within the overall system."

Keeping it simple was the biggest challenge, says Office design director Rob Alexander. When dealing with complicated problems, it's natural that some of the explorations would be visually complex. The Office team had to keep stripping them down to their simplest form. "During the design process, we were often asking ourselves how much can we remove and still get the idea across," he says.

Each week, the team presented a range of ideas to Ogilvy, whose team would then provide feedback and present its favorites to IBM. Once Ogilvy and the client had selected a concept, the design team would have a day to refine and finalize the design before it ran in a full-page ad in major newspapers around the world.

The icons also appeared on a website, online ads, billboards, airport ads, trade show exhibitions, and an IBM Smarter Planet attraction at Walt Disney World's Epcot Center.

Working on a project inspired by Rand was ideal for the Office team. "Rand is a design hero," says Schulte. "And the collaboration with the team at Ogilvy was rewarding. All of us felt good about being part of a campaign that's helping build a better world."

According to Ketchum and Godici, the campaign has been successfully provoking conversations about building a smarter planet, from classrooms, to boardrooms, to the White House.

"Eight days after being sworn into office, in his first major speech on the economy, President Barack Obama invited IBM Chairman Sam Palmisano to the White House to stand by him as he unveiled his plan to move the nation forward. With the launch of Smarter Planet, IBM turned a mandate for change into a mandate for smart," says Ketchum.

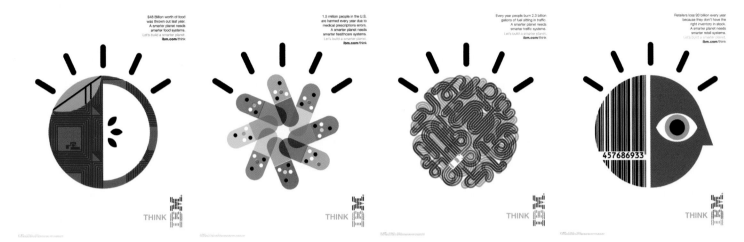

The icons/illustrations are shown here in posters.

IBM Smarter Planet icons also became part of an attraction at Walt Disney World's Epcot Center. (The exhibit was not designed by Office.)

826 Valencia
Identity Redesign

Office, San Francisco, California

The Valencia 826 logo is simultaneously modern and of a pirate world. It's as if it was designed to appeal to buccaneers rather than just being about them.

If you find yourself in need of Peg Leg Oil, Captain Blackbeard's Beard Dye (color: black), or Scurvy BeGone pills, then set course for 826 Valencia Pirate Supply Store, San Francisco's only purveyor of buccaneer supplies.

Named for its address in San Francisco's Mission District, 826 Valencia, a nonprofit tutoring center for kids, was founded in 2002 by best-selling author Dave Eggers and educator Ninive Calegari. Upon learning that the space for their new youth center was zoned strictly for commercial use, they opened a pirate supply store to meet city regulations. Since then, the unconventional storefront, which features drawers of hidden treasures, a vat of lard, and trapdoors filled with surprises, has helped draw curious kids into its free tutoring programs held in the back.

The model has also helped fund the organization's programs and has been successfully replicated in seven cities around the country, including 826 Brooklyn's Super Hero Supply Store and 826 Boston's Bigfoot Research Center.

In 2008, San Francisco–based creative studio Office approached 826 Valencia to help it reinvigorate the pirate store. The pro bono project included creating a new identity and nearly fifty new products, posters, signage, and interactive ideas for the store.

"The pirate store was already a wildly imaginative, inspiring, interactive experience," says Jill Robertson, president of Office. "We needed to create a visually cohesive story that reflected that same sense of humor and delight."

The goal was to create an authentic experience for an eighteenth-century pirate who happened to walk into San Francisco today. "We tried to design something for pirates, rather than something about pirates," says Jason Schulte, creative director of Office.

The team started by developing a logo, which was something the store had never used before.

Nothing says "pirate" like a classic skull and crossbones. The Office team created many iterations of the mark to develop a proprietary, 826 version of the ubiquitous symbol—tough but not scary, and quirky but not cute. The typography was hand drawn with subtle flourishes that reflect bones and flags.

To achieve a sense of authenticity, team went out of their way to make sure nothing appeared computer generated. "We created everything by hand first, with pencil sketches and ink drawings," says Rob Alexander, design director, Office. "And then we didn't polish them too much once we brought them into the computer."

The Office team also developed a series of secondary marks, to use on products like T-shirts for kids. Reflecting the unexpected and fun spirit of the store, the numbers "826" are created with sea creatures, an anchor, and other pirate-related themes.

Selected products and posters are available at 826valencia.org/store. All proceeds directly benefit 826 Valencia's writing programs.

826 Valencia sells a range of pirate products, also designed by Office, whose sales help support the nonprofit organization. (Photographer: Vanessa Chu.)

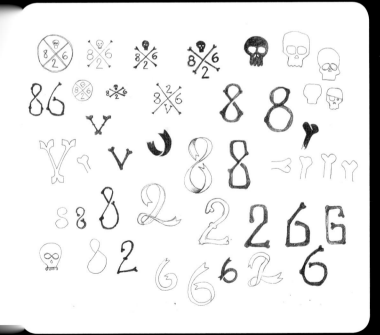

Sketches from Office's development of the Valencia 826 logo. It

This cast of characters were designed especially to be tough but not scary, and quirky but not cute.

Design Firm	MetaDesign
Client	Commerzbank
Project	Identity Design

The merger of Commerzbank and Dresdner Bank in May 2009 caused tremors throughout the financial system in Germany that few could have predicted.

In sheer size, the new organization was suddenly the second largest bank in Germany, just after Deutsche Bank. The merger was also a cultural phenomenon: Commerzbank and Dresdner were both very historic brands, comparable with Mercedes Benz. Commerzbank was founded in 1870, and Dresdner Bank in 1872; both had long been household brand names. Consumers and bank employees were understandably a bit unsettled in wondering what would happen to these familiar, trusted banks, and in turn, what would happen to their jobs, accounts, loans, and so on.

> When we started on the Commerzbank project, we thought of it as an opportunity to do a really historic redesign.

But making everyone even more nervous was the global financial crisis, which was ripening in 2009. Things were not going well. It appeared as if matters could only get worse.

In the middle of all of this angst was the design team at MetaDesign's Berlin office. When the two banks merged, the designers were already in the midst of an identity redesign for Commerzbank only. Suddenly, news of the merger was on the horizon. Now, two banks had to be considered in the redesign equation.

The financial crisis was hard enough on bank employees and bank customers, but adding the merger on top of malaise made the job of uniting the two banks and the people they represented that much more difficult.

"When we started on the Commerzbank project, we thought of it as an opportunity to do a really historic redesign. But then we had to bring together these companies and all of these people and establish a new idea that worked for everyone," says MetaDesign creative director, Thomas Klein. "People at the banks were confused and worried about their futures."

The clear direction for the design team was to bring the best aspects of both companies into a new identity. The new identity needed to reassure and motivate employees and customers alike. The first step would be to decipher what those best aspects were.

COMMERZBANK

Commerzbank's old logo used yellow as its corporate color. Its design was simple: Four arrows surround a central point.

Dresdner Bank
Die Beraterbank

Eine Marke der Commerzbank AG

The Dresdner brand had an emotionally charged history. Its logo was called "the eye of Ponto," after its beloved and well-trusted former chairman, Jürgen Ponto.

The new Commerzbank logo and wordmark is an elegant and effective combination of two existing German brands, preserving equity from each yet creating a strong new presence.

Commerzbank had long been overshadowed by Deutsche Bank, which had fantastic recognition as a global performer. Commerzbank did not have that same recognition as a strong personality driving forward toward the next successful deal.

But what it did have on the positive side was a reputation for having excellent character and of being a good partner to its customers. That feeling of trustworthy partnership needed to be maintained. The concept of stronger performance—which the merger would provide—needed to be added to the mix.

"This combination makes the new bank unique, because in Germany only Commerzbank combines partnership with performance," says Klein.

Commerzbank's existing logo used yellow as its corporate color. Its design was simple: Four arrows surround a central point. The logo could be read as a sunrise, as people or ideas coming together, or simply as a common goal. Its actual origin sprang from a much earlier merger of four banks into one: It was commonly referred to as "the four winds."

The Dresdner brand had an emotionally charged history. Its logo was called "the eye of Ponto," after its beloved and well-trusted former chairman,

Jürgen Ponto. Ponto was murdered in a failed Red Army Faction (RAF) kidnapping scheme in July 1977.

The employees of Dresdner, and by extension its customers, had a very deep identification with their brand and logo—a simple triangle set inside a green pentagon—and they strongly related to the brand. Abandoning that mark completely would mean abandoning some very valuable equity as well as upsetting many people.

The designers carefully considered concepts that would truly be a coming together of two equals. What eventually emerged was a very evenhanded mix: The Commerzbank name and the Dresdner bank logo were brought together in a deft weave.

"The new branding clearly symbolizes the ongoing integration of the two banks, both internally and externally," Klein explains. "The new mark, which combines elements of both banks in a contemporary manner, is a visible sign of the new Commerzbank. At the same time, the branding is in harmony with the bank's overall strategy. The new Commerzbank vision is to become the best bank in Germany, and in order to achieve this goal, we have sharpened the focus of the brand positioning."

A selection of collateral showing the new Commerzbank logo in use

The new branding clearly symbolizes the ongoing integration of the two banks, both internally and externally. The new mark, which combines elements of both banks in a contemporary manner, is a visible sign of the new Commerzbank.

The new trademark consists of three elements: the name "Commerzbank" in a new font, the color yellow, and the three-dimensional ribbon.

The three-dimensionality in "the eye of Ponto" emphasized the modern and sophisticated nature of the design. Additionally, the infinite loop of the sign in the eye stands for the ongoing dialog between customer, partner, and consultants of the new bank.

Commerzbank's house font is Compatil, which has a professional, modern look. It is the unifying element across all modes of the organization's communication. The interplay between the two font families of Compatil Text (serif) and Compatil Fact (sans serif) provides a design bandwidth that is capable of meeting all of the requirements of effective financial communication.

Strong brands are more than just logos and brand promises, says Klein. "They are a harmonious system of colors, visual worlds, and font types which serve to create a unified and consistent brand identity. A coherent corporate design increases the recognition and uniqueness of our brand. This is the best way to let the power of the new Commerzbank unfold.

"Now the identity has a new image, but the old brands are still there," he adds. "The logo is a merger of equals, from an identity perspective. We feel it is very successful for the look and feel of the new group, but it is possibly even more important for the motivation of the employees and the future of the bank. The people of the banks feel that they were not just taken over. We realize that this was very helpful for the whole community and for the new culture."

23andMe
Identity Design

MetaDesign, San Francisco, California

The main 23andMe logo creates a personable, approachable identity for a company that deals with very complex medical issues.

Say the words "personal genomics" to most people, and you'll probably get a blank stare in return. But personal genomics is a mind-expanding and meaningful new field of genetic study that allows individuals to learn more about their personal genomes through an easy, noninvasive test so that they can make smarter life choices.

23andMe is a personal genomics company that was founded in 2007 to provide a simple service. Basically, a customer uses a spit kit to provide a DNA sample to the company, and 23andMe returns practical information that applies directly to that person's life, hopefully to improve it. The service is personable, scientific, bright, and slightly audacious: The company needed a brand identity that matched that personality. The identity also needed to explain visually what the company does.

MetaDesign's San Francisco office developed the client's bright new identity. The designers knew that the brand needed to be scientific but not clinical, personable but not chatty. Customers needed to feel that the client was trustworthy and approachable. Bold color would help differentiate 23andMe from the starkness that pervades the visual landscape of health care and pharmaceuticals.

MetaDesign's director of strategy, Sean Ketchem, explains the final design and its many iterations.

"We based the logo on the idea of the human chromosome and the twenty-three chromosomes that inspired the company name. We created twenty-three unique versions of the identity using color and layout variations that express how even small variations, such as that within your genes, can result in something unique," he says.

A single version is used consistently as a lockup with the company name, but the different color and pattern variations can be used across applications to create variety in print pieces and on the Internet.

The forms in the logo represent chromosomes; their many and varied transparent colors show again and again the unique creations that new combinations form. Every one—that is, everyone—is different.

"The bright colors enliven the often intimidating complexities of personal genetics with personable, colorful forms, while the silver type expresses the scientific precision and rigor of the company," Ketchem explains.

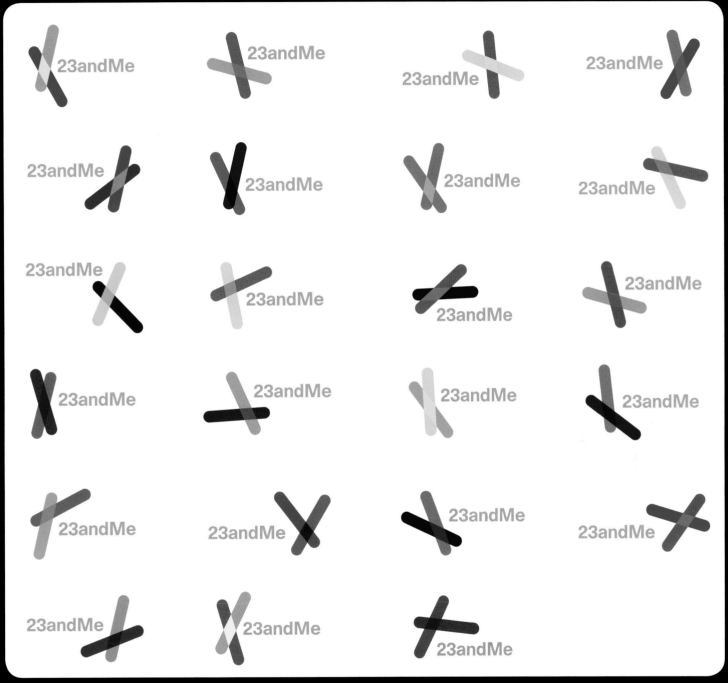

The entire suite of 23andMe logos contains twenty-three variations, representing the contents of the human chromosome and the many differences among peoples.

Design Firm	FutureBrand
Client	The Asian Cup 2011
Project	Identity Design

Held only once every four years, the Asian Cup is a football competition that raises extreme passions and hopes for fans and national teams alike. It attracts the attention of literally billions of fans around the world. The winning team is honored as the prestigious champion of Asia, and it automatically qualifies for the FIFA Confederation Cup.

But there are other honors to be had as well. The 2011 Asian Cup will be held in Doha in Qatar January 7–29, 2011. The Qatar Football Association in conjunction with the AFC sought to host the 2011 Cup not only for the recognition and business it would bring the country, but also in the hopes that a successful event would elevate the country so that it would be in the running for consideration for hosting the World Cup in 2022.

> The client's positioning statement included the following aspects: Arabic, competition, spirit, sportsmanship, and excitement.

So, everything that Qatar did in presenting the 2011 Asian Cup—organization, promotion, performance, and logistics—had to show that it could be a world-class venue. For help in creating the identity and marketing for the 2011 Cup, the QFA group contacted FutureBrand's Dubai office.

FutureBrand designers knew from the start that one idea unites football fans worldwide: goal. The new identity would need to speak of the host country, but it would also have to convey the sense of speed, excitement, world-class talent, and pride in performance that would enrich the Asian Cup games.

FutureBrand creative director Mark Thwaites says the client's positioning statement included the following aspects: Arabic, competition, spirit, sportsmanship, and excitement. His team's first round of logo trials dialed these attributes up and down in various combinations in what they called an identity exploration quilt. The quilt was still for in-house use only, to help them zero in on the strongest directions.

From the exploration quilt, the designers selected thirteen and then nine specific directions to present to the client. "The designs were selected because they provided a wide spectrum of potential ideas that all achieved the attributes and positioning," says Thwaites. "They all

The logo for The Asian Cup in Qatar 2011, created by FutureBrand, is an exciting combination of the soccer ball, the globe, the oryx (the national animal of Qatar), the region of Qatar, and the excitement of football.

achieved the desired attributes with different levels of youth appeal or pure football appeal."

The final nine were narrowed down to three. The feeling of motion and excitement in the ball-in-net logo had the right feeling, but perhaps didn't say as much about Qatar. The lowercase design did better: It achieved the desired attributes, had strong positive and negative balance, and was completely appropriate for the region, says Thwaites.

But the crossed oryxes contained everything the client wanted—country, Arabic, color, speed, gracefulness, two entities competing, all coming together in an abstracted soccer ball.

"The two oryxes crossing became the two teams competing," explains Thwaites. "This one had the right sense of national feeling. But it still had some problems with symmetry and with positive and negative space. The ball looked more like cracked ice than a soccer ball."

So, the team took the chosen design and moved it into refinement, where it was simplified and the type was tweaked to better integrate it.

As the design was simplified, the stronger Arabic attributes were dialed down. Line quality and color would add these qualities back in the next stage of refinement.

This exploration quilt shows the very wide range of approaches that FutureBrand designers created at the start of the project. Many of their experiments involved the oryx, a large antelope with swept-back horns that is the national animal of Qatar.

Some design trials, such as these, were very simple and clean.

The experiments below are based on the concept of looking down from a satellite view of the event, revealing the many people who would attend.

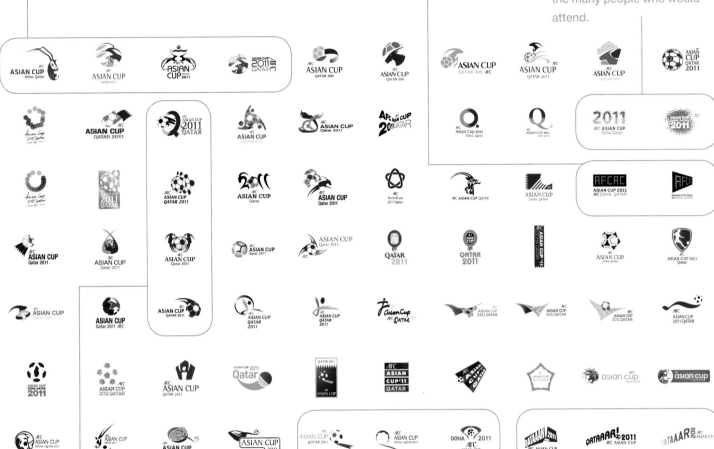

Other trials explored movement, such as the ball in motion or hitting the net.

This group represents some more literal concepts, where basic ideas such as the Q are presented simply.

These logos were built from a sound—the rallying cry issued by the football announcer when he says, "GOOOOALLL!"

From the exploration quilt, the most promising thirteen directions were selected (far right). From that group, FutureBrand narrowed the choices down to nine, and then finally three that were presented to the client, who selected the design shown at far left.

Refining the selected mark meant working out the delicate interplay between positive and negative space. As the designers fine-tuned the logo, aspects of Qatar, the animals, the soccer ball, and the world were dialed up and down.

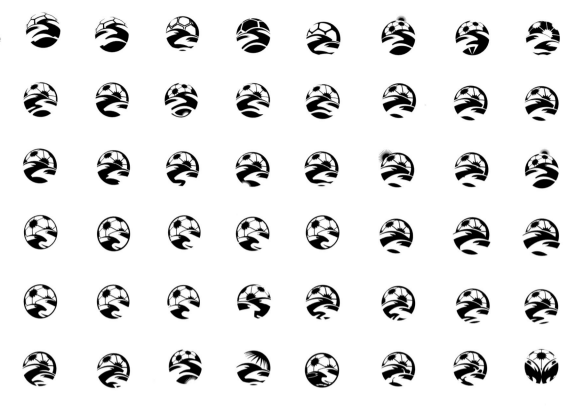

With the design finalized, the designers turned their attention to color selection. Qatar's national colors are maroon and white, so they were natural choices. But the designers also wanted to convey excitement and energy with brighter colors.

Thwaites notes that it was important for the team to remember to not be overly Arabic, because that would not represent the entire Middle Eastern fan base well. The logo would have to appeal to fans/customers from Korea and Australia, as well, to name just a few participant countries.

The designers also conducted plenty of color studies, gauging warm and cool colors while trying to integrate Qatar's national colors of maroon and white. Although they wanted to convey plenty of excitement and energy through their color choices, they also had to be careful to not let color combinations get too playful and childlike.

The final design is an ideal identity and solution for the client, says Thwaites. "It's a beautifully balanced mark that captures the essence of the host country and also has the attributes that make football known as a beautiful game. The typography works well with the mark, and the integration of the oryx and global football creates a balanced mark," he says.

The Asian Cup logo contains several extendable elements. The oryxes (below) are intriguing and suggest very rapid movement. Above are "motion rings" that mimic the logo's shape, color, and gradations.

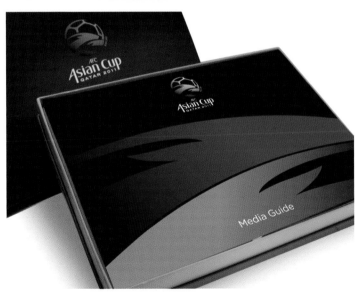

Several documents that show the identity system in use

Sergio Garcia
Identity Design

FutureBrand

In the past few years, it has become increasingly common for professional golfers to develop their own brand—not necessarily to imprint on their own goods, but to use as personal monograms for products produced by sponsors such as Nike and Adidas, for example.

FutureBrand worked with golfer Sergio Garcia to develop a personal imprint in 2009. His was a fortunate instance: Like Madonna or Prince, he was readily identifiable (in golf circles at least) by one name. He was widely known for his charming smile and bold manner of play. The FutureBrand team discovered he had many other valuable characteristics as well.

"The torque of his swing twists him almost into a pretzel; it has a very spiral nature. He is also known for a devilish sense of humor, and he is also very Spanish-centric—some would call him the ultimate Spaniard," explains Mark Thwaites, creative director for FutureBrand.

The design team also benefited in that the letter S was a very strong shape. As they began to work, they could see that the

S and the G could easily be combined into a distinctly new, twisting shape.

They presented seven very different ideas to the golfer. He particularly liked two of the directions, one very Gothic in nature and the other more modern but still with plenty of variation in stroke width. From those two, he finally selected the modern S/G combination.

The designers then took the basic idea and moved it into refinement, where it underwent some dramatic changes. More of the Gothic traits that Garcia liked were brought back in, as was a sense of playfulness.

"Some of the letters are almost hornlike. They're very devilish. It's sort of like a tattoo in some ways," says Thwaites. "The final logo feels very Spanish, with even the colors of the Spanish flag. It has a lot of things wrapped up in it, and the most beautiful story. It has very rich attributes that got combined in a very simple, reproducible way. Simplicity can tell the most amazing stories."

Design Firm	Porkka-Kuutsa
Client	Indufor
Project	Identity Redesign

People depend on forests, and forests depend on the decisions that people make. A sustainable balance, now and in the future, requires knowledge, skill, and commitment.

These simple principles form the foundation of Indufor's operations. Indufor is a global, independently owned company based in Finland that gathers and analyzes information from forests for private and governmental clients involved in such industries as furniture, papermaking, lumber, construction, and more. These clients need forest products for current as well as future profits, so they are very interested in sustainability. Indufor helps them make wise decisions that will carry them profitably into the future.

> The former identity didn't reflect the crisp expertise and knowledge the staff at Indufor has, or the high quality and in-depth services that the company provides.

In fact, Indufor's name is formed from the words *industry* and *forest*, two seemingly disparate concepts. "Indufor's expertise is to combine sustainable values with economic opportunities to find the best solution for both society and nature without compromising the environment," says Jonni Kuutsa, partner in Porkka-Kuutsa (Helsinki).

"Indufor had a somewhat convoluted visual identity before our work," says Kuutsa. "The former identity didn't reflect the crisp expertise and knowledge the staff at Indufor has, or the high quality and in-depth services that the company provides to industry, NGOs, and government agencies, such as the UN. It lacked emotion, direction, and consistency, and moreover, it needed a complete visual overhaul," Kuutsa explains. Porkka-Kuutsa partnered with input & output (Thomas Barbieri) to create Indufor's new visual identity, graphic guidelines, and signature (logo).

Most of Indufor's competitors are bigger consulting groups that operate in many business areas besides forest consulting. "What makes Indufor different and unique compared to other forest-related consultancy agencies is that its core business is focused on forests and the environment," says Kuutsa.

The new logo for Indufor Oy, a company that collects forest intelligence worldwide, created by Porkka-Kuutsa (Helsinki)

Indufor's original logo said nothing about the company's expertise, nor did it have any emotional content or even say much about its role in advising on the natural world.

Because Indufor's core business deals with forests, the design team started the redesign by considering related themes such as trees, leaves, and so on. But because varieties of trees and forests are so different in various parts of the world—for instance, the eucalyptus tree alone has more than 700 species—any specific leaf, bark, trunk, or tree shape image they might have selected would be too restrictive for a global identity. So, this idea was abandoned, in part.

Another attribute the client wanted to include in the new identity was Indufor's global presence. This led naturally to a globe-shaped logo, a globe as seen from space. But the designers still wanted to somehow bring in the images of trees.

They developed an intriguing bar effect that could represent both the globe and trees. Blue is used to represent the globe, and green bars represent forests and trees (trunks). The design team selected natural, fresh hues, and surrounded them with black to represent space.

"The blue and green striping effect can be used in several ways. For instance, it can be laid over photos of almost any kind so that the client (Indufor) has flexibility in presentations, documents, and so on, while rebranding themselves with their new visual identity. The combination makes Indufor unique, incorporating forests, the world, and the environment. The transparency in the colors is symbolic of the company's transparency in its operations," says Kuutsa.

A set of sketches from Porkka-Kuutsa's design trials shared the same natural palette, but most centered on organic shapes such as leaves. However, representing any specific leaf shape made the logo too specific.

The new identity compared with the old shows a much more interesting and dramatic presentation. In the new version, the use of a photo behind the identity is demonstrated.

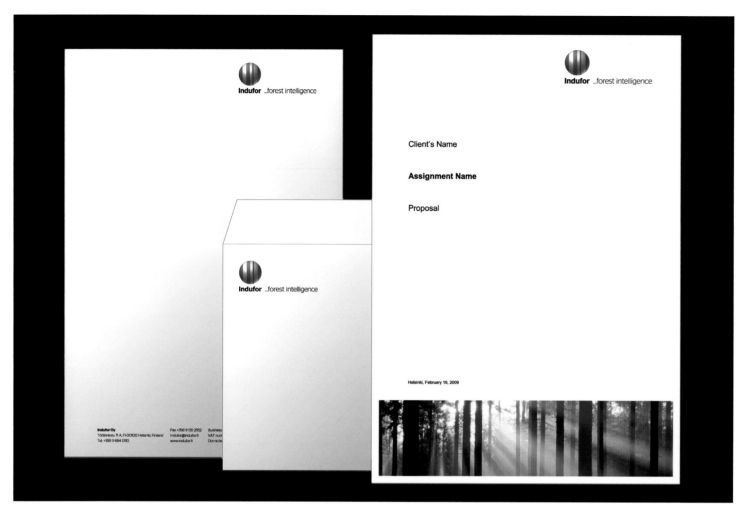

The designers specified the Stag Sans family because it is modern and reader-friendly, and it offers a wide family to choose from. "Moreover, the Stag Sans font with its rounded edges is symbolic of the roundness of the globe," says Kuutsa.

The slogan, "Indufor . . . forest intelligence," as well as the new logo, are successful because they are solidly based on three fundamental elements that the company incorporates in all its work.

Barbieri explains: "Analytical intelligence = reasoning, processing information, and solving problems/issues. Indufor conducts analyses, evaluates, judges, and compares. Creative intelligence = utilizes past experiences to achieve insights to deal selectively, effectively, and efficiently with situations and/or areas of operation worldwide. And practical intelligence = the way in which Indufor's people have the ability to select, adapt, and shape the best and most appropriate solutions in which clients benefit, not only economically, but including social and environmental responsibly exercising sound stewardship and international legislation."

The new identity is endlessly adaptable, no matter what part of the world Indufor needs to represent or work with: Photos from forests from anywhere in the world can be used behind the bar system.

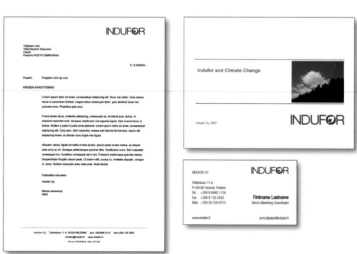

The old and new letterhead systems

The old and new identities used in an Indufor publication. The client is still able to use lush photos of forests, but superimposing the bar identity adds the Indufor message.

The new identity shown on a business card and an information card

URV Foundry
Identity Design,

Porkka-Kuutsa, Helsinki, Finland

URV Foundry (from the full name, Uudenkaupungin Rautavalimo) is a Finnish company that produces ductile and gray iron castings. The production specializes on single and short series castings with weights ranging from 20 to 6,000 kg/pc for power plants, the marine industry, wind turbines, the lift and elevator industry, and the pulp and paper industry.

Porkka-Kuutsa was contacted to create a new signature to reflect URV's worldwide business activities in a modern and fresh way.

"URV has a good reputation in the machine building industry, but its former signature was dull in appearance and lacked the dynamic and hot look it now has," says Jonni Kuutsa, a partner at the design firm. "Moreover, URV produces objects with very interesting shapes, forms, and angles."

Porkka-Kuutsa studied the company, its products, its clients, and the end-users of its products. "We started out by focusing on a ball shape that combined the shape of a cast object—a valve—coupled with the letter *U*. As time progressed, the round shape also suggested the globe, which reflects URV's customers, supply systems, and global presence," says Antti Porkka, also a partner at the design firm.

At URV, the iron is cast into shapes by first melting it in a furnace. The liquid metal is poured into a mold, and then the casting is removed after the iron has solidified as it cools. "The heat in the foundry helped us to select the logo colors of warm yellow and orange shades for the identity," Kuutsa explains.

"The holes in the logo ball create a feeling of a technically complicated and demanding iron casting, coupled with the globe," he says. "We selected the Slab Serif typeface to create a technical and mechanical feeling. But the face is still usable as the company's main typeface," says Kuutsa.

The logo is not animated as of this writing, but Kuutsa says that it could be done easily in the future.

The old and new URV identities. The new identity is based on the image/shape of a metal casting, representing the client's work, and it subtly reveals the letter U.

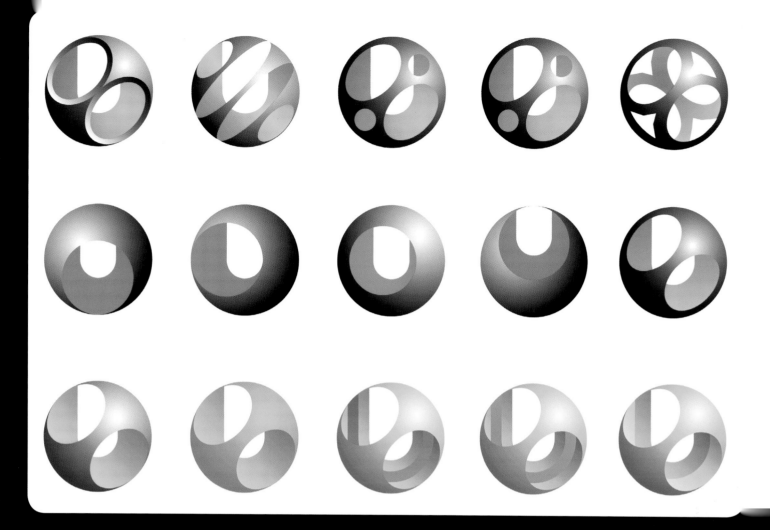

Above: A series of sketches that Porkka-Kuutsa created for URV, using the casting as a foundation

Left: Porkka-Kuutsa built a very warm orange and yellow palette for the client based on the extreme heat necessary to produce castings from molten metal.

Design Firm	Landor
Client	The Public-Private Partnership for Handwashing with Soap
Project	Identity Design

Landor's identity design for Global Handwashing Day (GHD) is a study in contrasts. The design was meant to inspire the humblest of human actions—washing one's hands with soap and water—but it had to spread that notion worldwide. Its goal was to save thousands of lives, but it was aimed squarely at the smallest among us, the young child.

The design firm had become involved in the project through its connection to client Procter & Gamble. P&G is a partner with the World Bank, the Water and Sanitation Program, UNICEF, USAID, the Centers for Disease Control and Prevention, and Unilever in the Public-Private Partnership for Handwashing with Soap (PPPHW), an organization with a simple goal: to dramatically reduce deaths around the world due to disease caused by

> Our job was to cause a change that would transform handwashing with soap from an abstract idea into an automatic behavior.

poor or inadequate hygiene. The group had many directions it could pursue to achieve this goal—point-of-use water treatment, sanitation, and hygiene education, for example—but the effort that would yield the greatest degree of benefit most efficiently and cost-effectively was handwashing with soap. P&G, a leader in advocating the power of design, reached out to Landor as a strategic partner. Landor's global reach and long-term history taking insight and transforming it into design that connects with P&G consumers around the world made them the partner of choice.

"Part of the problem is that in some developing countries, people don't understand that soap is a necessary part of handwashing. Our job was to cause a change that would transform handwashing with soap from an abstract idea into an automatic behavior," says Adam Waugh, senior designer in Landor's Cincinnati office.

That critical change would yield astounding results. "Thousands of kids can be saved per day just by washing with soap," says Gerhard Koenderink, executive creative director, also in the Cincinnati office. Diarrheal diseases and pneumonia kill almost two million children each year, making them the second leading killers of children worldwide, according to the World Health Organization.

Global Handwashing Day
October 15

Global Handwashing Day is a worldwide initiative aimed to reduce disease and death by turning effective handwashing into an automatic behavior for all people. Its identity was created by Landor Associates.

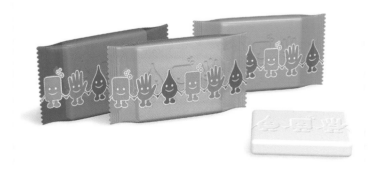

Top: The logo for Global Hand-washing Day started with a wide variety of trials submitted from Landor offices in Sydney, London, Hong Kong, Dubai, and Mexico City. The Landor team leaders were looking for ideas that unmistakably communicated handwashing with soap at first glance. The communication tone needed to be warm, educational, direct, and simple.

This is the first page of sketches from the various offices. The seed of the final solution can be seen on the far left of the page.

Center: A second page of design trials from various Landor offices

Bottom: A third page of experiments

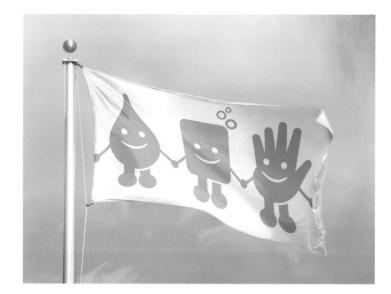

The brief for the GHD identity project indicated that the effort needed a strong visual identity that could be instantly understood by people in any country, even by those who were illiterate. It needed to communicate quickly and appeal to adults and children. The new identity also had to work in a range of media and for any size of budget, and it had to avoid offending by concept, image, or color in all cultures.

"To change the way people act, you have to find the simplest way of making the biggest change in their lives," explains Koenderink. "Many times, and around the world, kids are the ones who bring new information to the family. So, this effort really was from the bottom up."

The identity also had to appeal to governments and leaders around the world. "We needed their advocacy in the communities. We created the teaching tools, and it was up to them to implement," adds Waugh.

As soon as Landor's Cincinnati office gathered all of the necessary information, Koenderink and Waugh sent it out to Landor's offices in Sydney, London, Hong Kong, Dubai, and Mexico City. Each office was given six days to submit ideas and sketches, all of which would be considered as solutions.

Koenderink and Waugh were looking for ideas that unmistakably communicated handwashing with soap at first glance. The communication tone needed to be warm, educational, direct, and simple. Solutions were presented on a range of rational, emotional, and experiential attributes.

The remainder of this article visually tracks the path of the project.

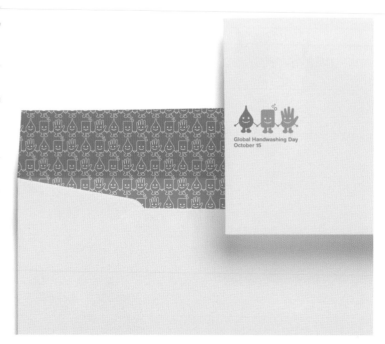

Clean hands save lives

Handwashing with Soap: The Basics

2

erm, Global Handwashing
ome a powerful platform
aimed at policy makers
keholders and an occasion
public commitment to
will spur behavior change.

Reduction in diarrheal morbidity
per invention type

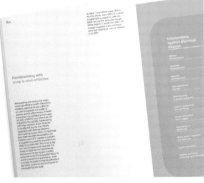

15 October

We did it!

15 October marks the annual Global Handwashing Day-
it is a hygiene-related, recurring event that revolves around
schools and children. Organized by a partnership between
public organizations and private partners to promote
handwashing with soap, this important campaign faces
a challenge to transform handwashing with soap from
an abstract "good idea" into an automatic behavior
performed in homes, schools, and communities worldwide.

Global Handwashing Day was initiated in 2008 by the
Global Public-Private Partnership for Handwashing with
Soap, and it is endorsed by a wide array of governments,
international institutions, civil society organizations, NGOs,
private companies, and individuals around the globe.

A variety of applications for the Global
Handwashing Day identity. The characters in the logo are easily translat-
able into print or three-dimensional
objects such as soap or toys.

9/11 Memorial
Identity Design

Landor, New York, New York

The new 9/11 Memorial identification, created by Landor Associates

Few events are more visually charged than the day of September 11, 2001. Everyone has a picture, a memory, a moment that will stay with him or her always. Just the mention of the numbers 9/11 brings it back instantly.

That is perhaps why the name "The National September 11 Memorial & Museum at the World Trade Center" didn't particularly resonate well with the public, although it does describe the nonprofit organization. It operates, programs, raises funds for, and oversees the memorial and museum, currently under construction for completion in 2011, but its name was too wordy to evoke the immediacy and emotion of the day.

Since 2007, the organization was represented by a purple and gray lockup that contained representations of the two reflecting pools that are planned for the site, with the lengthy name at its center. The gradients in the pools made them difficult to reproduce, especially at smaller sizes, and overall, the design looked grim and static, not hopeful and forward-looking.

In 2009, the group contacted Landor for assistance in implementing its unwieldy name. Rietje Gieskes, associate design director for the project, recalls that the design firm promptly suggested shortening the fifty-eight-character name which resulted in the shorthand name, 9/11 Memorial.

"We tried to consider the images of that day. Everyone in the studio felt very close to the project. There are many visuals that come to mind, but we needed a new icon based on a singular image. If you say '9/11,' you picture the towers. It became apparent that that was the obvious and appropriate choice," she says.

The pools-as-logo were not evocative because their image is not something people know yet. "In this case it seemed important to use an image that people were already familiar with instead of creating a new one. The reflecting pools may be associated with the site in the future, but are not now."

Whatever the Landor team created, it had to work with Gotham, a typeface already heavily in use by the organization. For the new logo, they chose Verlag, a face that has a sense of the sophistication of New York. The font works well with Gotham and has an austere, timeless feel, which was extremely important given the simplicity of the numerals: Its design doesn't overshadow what it represents in the logo.

That being said, the numerals were substantially altered to make sure the entire design was balanced, that each character was compatible, and that they were bold enough in black or reverse.

Finding the right blue for the design also took time. "Everyone always says how blue the sky was that day," Gieskes says. "We tried to incorporate that with the right sense of hope and stature. The blue could not be too cyan or too navy."

Since the new mark has been in use since August 2009, the client, the public, and even the mayor of New York have embraced it.

"It's forward looking," Gieskes says of the strong, two-pillared design. "A horrible thing happened, but as people rebuild their lives, there must be hopefulness."

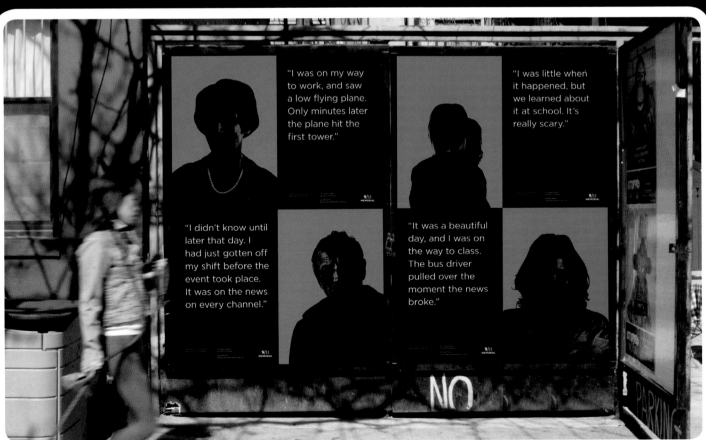

Design Firm	Gee + Chung
Client	National Semiconductor Corporation
Project	Brand Identity Design

National Semiconductor Corporation of Santa Clara, California, is one of the world's leading analog chipmakers. The company's SolarMagic technology is a proprietary brand of power optimizer that maximizes the energy output of solar photovoltaic panel systems in a revolutionary way.

Current solar power solutions consist of solar panels connected to inverters, which change direct current into alternating current for household or commercial use. The SolarMagic power optimizer is a small converter box between the panels and inverter in the system that can recoup up to 57 percent of the power that is lost to less-than-ideal situations, such as shade and irregular panel performance. This recapturing of power significantly improves an owner's return on investment and makes installation possible in many other less-than-ideal sites.

Having already designed National Semiconductor's industry-leading PowerWise brand of energy-efficient chips, Earl Gee and Fani Chung of Gee + Chung Design (San Francisco) were asked to also develop the client's SolarMagic brand of solar converter/power optimizer technology.

The primary audience for the SolarMagic brand included solar installers and solar panel manufacturers, aged eighteen to fifty-five and predominately male. Key geographic sales areas included North America (California, Arizona, Nevada, Oregon, and New Jersey), Europe (Germany, Italy, and Spain), Japan, and China. The secondary audiences included financial analysts, industry reporters, semiconductor engineers, and government agencies.

The primary marketing objectives of the SolarMagic brand were to position National as an innovative, creative technology leader in delivering system solutions, and as the leader in energy-efficiency design. As the first mover in the solar panel power optimizer market, the new brand had no immediate competition, although competitors were anticipated in the next three to five years.

The single most important advantage the brand has over other systems is that the SolarMagic converter enhances the performance of each panel, allowing it to achieve maximum efficiency under adverse conditions, while existing solutions do not. The client wanted the new SolarMagic identity to represent the qualities of "innovative," "cutting-edge technology," and "easy to use." The brand should not convey "commodity item," "expensive," or "complicated."

National Semiconductor, one of the world's leading analog chipmakers, develops a brand of innovative solar conversion technology which transforms solar energy into electric current by multiplying the power of the sun. The progression of emanating silicon wafers in perspective symbolizes the transformative nature of the company's power optimizer technology, using alternating yellow and blue colors to represent the conversion and optimization of solar input to electrical output.

"The SolarMagic brand was successful in conveying the innovative and transformative nature of National's power optimizer technology and in establishing an entirely new product category within the industry," says Gee.

In this article, we are sharing Gee + Chung Design's actual presentation to National Semiconductor, to share the project's story as well as the presentation's look and feel.

The design firm was very fortunate to work with an extremely astute, talented, and dedicated team at National, including Todd D. Whitaker, vice president, Worldwide Marketing Operations; Jocelyn King, director, Worldwide Marketing Operations; and HoMan Lee, design manager, Brand Management & Advertising/Corporate Marketing. The National team was instrumental in making the case for the SolarMagic brand's attributes to senior management and throughout the company to enable a highly successful launch.

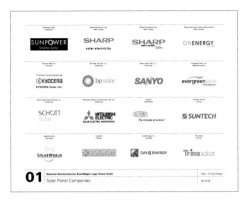

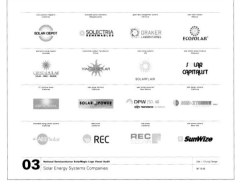

Gee + Chung Design began its process with a thorough visual audit. They examined existing identities, conceptual directions, and visual trends within the client's circle of business to identify opportunities that would differentiate the SolarMagic brand. The categories reviewed included everything from solar panel companies to solar energy conferences, as well as SolarMagic brands (companies with the same name but not in the client's industry).

The designers found that while the majority of solar energy companies utilize sun imagery to communicate solar energy, solar panels, or solar energy systems, very few companies went further in conveying additional qualitative attributes. This presented an important strategic opportunity for the client to conceptually represent the process of solar conversion and the qualities of a cutting-edge, breakthrough technology that is easy to use.

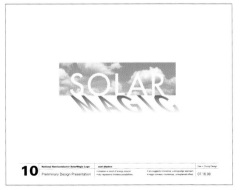

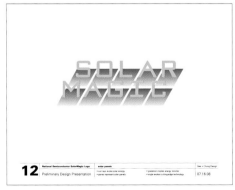

Preliminary Design The designers developed a list of key messages based on National's answers to the creative brief (top left). They explored several options in their first round of designs, trying to explore as many brand attributes as possible in the most compelling manner, constantly checking design solutions against the key messages list to determine effectiveness. Each concept in the presentation was assigned a number and descriptive name, with its attributes listed underneath for easy reference. Five representative slides from the presentation are shown here.

Design Refinement While refining the most promising directions selected by the client, the designers explored several new and equally promising directions that they felt should be reviewed. From extensive experience meeting extremely tight deadlines during the dot-com period, Gee + Chung Design sometimes had to proceed with the Design Refinement phase before they would have liked. This time around, they were determined to present the client with the most effective ideas possible within this project's very short time frame. As it turned out, the most compelling direction, Multiplying Power Sun, emerged from this additional exploration. Below are sample representative slides from that presentation.

Final Design The creation of the final signature involved the resolution of several important issues, including creating the most effective scale progression within the logo, providing the optimal letterspacing and relationship of the logo to logotype, designating the appropriate clear area around the logo, and defining the most legible usage of the logo on color backgrounds.

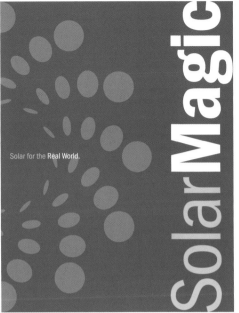

Applications The designers applied the SolarMagic logo to stationery, trucks, and an animated intro. With each component, the designers tried to discover new ways to conceptually extend the ideas behind the brand and create a graphically compelling piece.

The letterhead splits the logo in half, as a screened-back pattern on the front and alternating color on the back. The envelope uses the logo on a yellow background with a bold, eye-catching flap. The business card employs a unique die-cut to highlight the logo and create additional panels for marketing information.

The graphics use color in a flexible manner to define the truck's different surfaces, featuring a bright white side panel with a giant cropped logo, a yellow roll-up door, blue cab, yellow wheels, and custom mud flaps.

The launch intro for dealers and distributors features the logo dynamically spiraling into the frame and locking into position. The letterforms come together as a metaphor for the creation of a new technology. The logo constantly pulsates to represent the continuous conversion of solar energy to electric current.

DCM
Logo Designs
Gee + Chung Design, San Francisco, California

Gee + Chung Design has enjoyed a successful ten-year relationship with client DCM, a leading Silicon Valley venture capital company with significant investments in China, having designed everything from ads and corporate literature to its website and internal messaging. During that time, Earl Gee and Fani Chung have also had the opportunity to design a Lunar New Year logo for each of the four past years.

"DCM is the only U.S.-based venture capital firm to host its own Lunar New Year celebration in China to promote networking among its entrepreneurs and limited partners," says Gee. "The events demonstrate the firm's strong commitment to its technology ventures in China, and have been instrumental in establishing DCM as a leading global venture capital firm in China."

The centerpiece of each of the annual identities is a curious creature. The Dog, Boar, Rat, and Ox that the team created are on their surfaces traditional Chinese lunar calendar animals. But on closer inspection, some extraordinary illumination reveals itself. Each logo is designed using the firm's initials in the client's Clarendon Bold corporate font. Each letter, its size and case, were chosen to suggest physical attributes and sometimes pure whimsy.

"We started out by tracing different sized letterforms to create the general form and character of each animal. It was fun figuring out which combination of upper- and lowercase letters would best represent the individual features of each animal," says Gee. The effect is to convey DCM's bold, confident outlook for the firm's investments in China in the new year.

The logos were applied to a wide variety of Lunar New Year promotions, including the party invitations, greeting cards, gift bags, online invitations, and event banners.

"We selected New Page Centura Silk 100# Cover, being the highest-quality stock with the highest amount of recycled content available," says Gee. "Oscar Printing provided incredible attention to detail in producing the party invitations and greeting cards. Fong & Fong Printers and Lithographers printed the gift bags and

DCM, a leading Silicon Valley venture capital firm with significant investments in China, welcomes the Year of the Dog, Boar, Rat, and Ox, using the firm's initials to create proprietary Chinese lunar calendar animals and convey the firm's bold, confident outlook for its investments in China.

sourced the custom red and gold grommets and handles. We used metallic gold foil to evoke a festive, New Year appeal whenever possible, creating items that attendees would want to save as keepsakes of the event, or in the case of the gift bag, reuse."

DCM, recognizing that successful venture investing is built upon strong personal relationships, designed the Lunar New Year celebrations not as formal, "sit-down" Chinese banquets, but as informal receptions that would foster interaction and relationship building between the entrepreneur and investor attendees.

Each year's celebration has been extremely well received, and the events continue to attract a greater number of entrepreneurs and limited partners. The Lunar New Year campaigns have proved to be an effective extension of the DCM brand, and have been successful in establishing DCM as one of the preeminent U.S.-based venture capital firms in China.

The greeting card employs metallic gold foil to create a festive appeal. The gift bag conveys yin and yang through its wraparound motif and alternating color.

The online invitation uses animated letterforms to introduce the Lunar New Year animal.

Design Firm	BNA (Brand Nature Access)
Client	Empik
Project	Identity Redesign

Empik has sixty years of experience in the Polish market as a leading media and entertainment retailer, with 103 multimedia stores in Poland and 24 stores in the Ukraine. It offers an impressive selection of books, recordings, films, multimedia, stationery, and photo items—but so do many other international competitors such as Amazon, which in 2008 and 2009 was making serious online inroads into the Polish market.

Despite its many offerings and specialized knowledge of the Polish consumer, Empik's existing visual identity and in-store experience did not correspond with the age of the Internet. Its stores were overloaded with goods, and customers often felt disoriented and tired after shopping—some described Empik shops as "warehouses"—and said they would

The new Empik logo, by BNA (Brand Nature Access), Warsaw, Poland

> Many people recognized it—about 96 percent of Poles recognize the Empik brand—but the logo offered no suggestion of what the brand was.

rather do their shopping online and at home. This less-than-positive experience was causing customers to lose their loyalty to a historic and cultural brand that they had long been faithful to.

The Polish design studio BNA (Brand Nature Access, of Warsaw) was asked to help Empik reestablish that connection in a modern, intelligent way that would, over time, help Polish consumers fall in love again with the brand and feel more attached to it than they would any outside interloper. BNA felt it had a solid case in establishing its client as the go-to brand: In 2008, eBay had been driven out of the country by the already established Polish brand Allegro. So, BNA knew that cultural loyalty could be an effective tool in the redesign.

The original Empik logo had outlived its usefulness. But as about 96 percent of Poles recognize the Empik brand, it had exceptional equity.

The original Empik logo was difficult to explain, says BNA president, Mariusz Przybyl.

"It was very old fashioned, and not in a good sense. And the brand had nothing to do with being vintage. The logo showed a ball going through the lettering of the name, like it was some sort of magic or fantasy. It was strange, but it was also very characteristic. Many people recognized it—about 96 percent of Poles recognize the Empik brand—but the logo offered no suggestion of what the brand was," Przybyl says of the thirty-year-old mark.

The apostrophe is more like a brand property. It's really not a logo as much as an art element that you can use in many different ways.

To move the store brand from being seen as a warehouse to being embraced by shoppers, a new Empik brand mission was written. It included these attributes:

• Easy, unlimited access to the whole world
• Giving the pleasure of discovery
• Joyful guidance through the labyrinth of culture
• Faith in human creation
• Entertainment as the most human expression
• Disseminating the mindset of openness, understanding, optimism, tolerance, and joy
• Understanding the variety, diversity, and complexity of life, cultures, and creative attitudes
• Infecting others with the fascination for knowledge
• Explaining the meaning of cultural phenomena
• Free individual expression as the basis of culture
• A sense of humor

Because the client wanted the brand to speak in a more relevant way to consumers, the BNA team decided to conduct a personality audit of what Empik aspired to be. Among the traits that were discovered were these: wise, enlightened, a good sense of humor, Polish, cosmopolitan, young, has traveled abroad, straightforward, confident but humble, helpful, mellow, creative, classic in appearance, provocative, and eloquent.

"We even conjectured what the handwriting of this person would be like. We discovered a very literate person who speaks a lot about his discoveries of the whole world. This was the most important thing to design into the brand—that this person knows a lot and can speak of it," Przybyl says.

The design team began by working with the "rolling ball" from the old logo. It was easy to parlay into new visuals—of a hat, a ball of yarn, a pump handle, and more—but what made perfect sense with the new definition of the brand as an erudite, verbal person was an apostrophe, or more specifically, a single quote mark.

"The apostrophe is more like a brand property," says Przybyl. "It's really not a logo as much as an art element that you can use in many different ways."

The apostrophe or quote easily symbolizes the quoting of culture, of people talking and writing. It is the tool of writers, musicians, actors, and everyone else associated with culture and entertainment.

A new proprietary Empik typeface was designed by a leading Polish typographer, Lukasz Dziedzic. The face is simple, modern, and bold. It has a friendly, approachable feel, but feels definite and solid. Placing the apostrophe element in the store's name in the same place as the rolling ball element in the old logo established an immediate connection between the old and new identities.

The apostrophe element was immediately seized upon by BNA designers as the key element in the existing Empik identity. Here, they sketch out ways that the little mark could be used.

Above: The old Empik store presence was outdated and uninspiring. The store interior did not play off of the identity, nor did the logo or identity say anything about what the organization is all about.

Right: The new Empik identity is bold and distinctive, as shown by these two store exteriors. It is simple and modern, and the valuable apostrophe element sits very comfortably in the new logo.

The apostrophe/quote element and new typeface/identity system was put to use immediately in the store environment. The BNA team devised a layout and signage system that helped visitors move around easily and quickly find goods and products.

The designers also used the apostrophe/quote as an art element. In the stores, its shape can be used as a sign, or it can be repeated in posters as collage. In the future, they see it taking on surface treatments, too: It could be a thought bubble, a chunk of cheese, a hook about to be bitten by a fish, or just about anything else the Empik team might dream up.

The effect is to create a unified, understandable, and comfortable source for culture and entertainment, all under one roof. And the proof is in the numbers: Empik has enjoyed a 25 to 30 percent increase in sales per year since the new identity was implemented in 2008.

The brand implementation is still underway, and some stores are still being outfitted. It has been successful, Przybyl says, because of the attention to detail. "The system is special because of typography. It makes the identity work," he says.

Inside the Empik stores, the apostrophe element is used as art, as sculpture, and as an organizational agent. A bright color palette, combined with the new proprietary Empik typeface, produces a clean, distinct, and organized experience for the customer.

BPH Bank, GE Capital Group
Identity Design

BNA, Warsaw, Poland

In 2010, Bank BPH merged with GE Money Bank Poland and now operates under the name of BPH Bank, GE Capital Group (Poland). Both of the original banks had a different focus and customer group. Bank BPH focused on small and medium-size enterprises (SMEs), corporate accounts, and wealthy individual clients, while GE Money Bank focused on typical consumer-level finances.

The original banks were also very different in terms of their identity.

"GE Money benefited from using the familiar General Electric identity, while BPH used an identity that was very generic in terms of color—most financial institutions use blue and red in their identities here—and it aimed to communicate the values of dynamism and modernity," says Maja Malinowska, brand consultant with BNA, the design firm that created a new identity for the merged banks.

The new client was to be positioned as a "bank that plays fair."

"We were looking for a visual symbol that would show that the bank was a partner for the customer and that they had an equal relationship," explains Malinowska. "We were also looking for a visual concept which is capacious enough to talk about many aspects of the bank-client relationship."

As no elements had to be saved from either of the former identities, the BNA design team could and did begin fresh. They eventually decided on the concept of an unbroken line. It could be used as both an identity element and a way to illustrate the new bank's philosophies and activities. The line could form just about any illustration—of items, of people working together, and so on—and it could also be used in interior/exterior design, in print publications, and in other applications.

In the Bank BPH logo, the line is used to draw out two simple forms that represent the figures of the customer and banker, just touching in a simple, friendly manner.

"The unbroken line was both very clear as a cultural symbol of functioning hand in hand and it is an adaptable graphic motif," Malinowska says.

The designers decided to use the motif of blended colors as another visual symbol that demonstrates how the bank world and the customer world are combined at BPH. The mix of red and orange was distinctive to the banking category in Poland (where most use red and blue).

The original GE Money Bank and Bank BPH logos

collections and sketches

LOGO SEARCH

Keywords | Initials

Type: ○ Symbol ○ Typographic ○ Combo ● All

austin
CONVENTION CENTER

AFRICAN EYE
TELEVISION NETWORK

apetitoteca

ARCHIVAL
CLOTHING

actionlink

LUXURY
OF AUSTRIA

AQUABELLA

armtec
VISION | BUILT

A A L E X   O Y
Lakiasiaintoimisto Oleg Gusev

Anna
Kövecses

amc
TECHNOLOGIES

ANDREW SEIFERT
upright • electric bass

ⅅ = Design Firm   ⓒ = Client

A	B	C	D	
 Brandogolik	 VipbillinG	 moscowbase	 bgroup	1
	 BRANDTHESPEAKER	 Brunn		2
 Bride in a box				3
 BE THIRTEEN	 EMBARGO		 Book Worship™	4
 CHANTEST	 connecticut climate change		 cignias™	5

Ⓓ = Design Firm　Ⓒ = Client

1A Ⓓ Z&G Ⓒ Alexandr Kalganov　1B Ⓓ Cheltsov Ⓒ Vipbilling　1C Ⓓ Cheltsov Ⓒ Moscowbase　1D Ⓓ NoCo Ⓒ BGroup

2A Ⓓ Karl Design Vienna Ⓒ Bodalgo GmbH　2B Ⓓ Dreambox Creative Ⓒ Brand The Speaker　2C Ⓓ Davina Chatkeon Design Ⓒ Brunn Music　2D Ⓓ Roy Smith Design Ⓒ Roy Smith

3A Ⓓ Clay McIntosh Creative Ⓒ Bride In A Box　3B Ⓓ Phony Lawn Ⓒ Boulder Soupworks　3C Ⓓ Galperin Design, Inc. Ⓒ Bilski's　3D Ⓓ McGuire Design Ⓒ The Butcher Bros.

4A Ⓓ Designer? Ⓒ Client?　4B Ⓓ Logoholik Ⓒ Bojan Stefanovic　4C Ⓓ Greenhouse Studio Ⓒ BrrrBerry Frozen Yogurt　4D Ⓓ Hazen Creative, Inc. Ⓒ Self

5A Ⓓ Du4 Designs Ⓒ Chantest　5B Ⓓ Bertz Design Group Ⓒ Connecticut Climate Change / State of Connecticut　5C Ⓓ Roy Smith Design Ⓒ Creative Target　5D Ⓓ Ceb Design Ⓒ Cignias Inc.

	A	B	C	D
1				
2				
3				
4				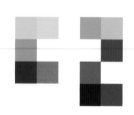
5				

Ⓓ = Design Firm   Ⓒ = Client

1A Ⓓ Pop Ovidiu Sebastian Ⓒ Comat   1B Ⓓ TypeOrange Ⓒ Available   1C Ⓓ Tran Creative Ⓒ Coeur d'Alene Golf Shop   1D Ⓓ Gardner Design Ⓒ Complete Landscaping Systems

2A Ⓓ Spring Advertising + Design Ⓒ Joey Restaurant Group   2B Ⓓ T&E Polydorou Design Ltd Ⓒ Michalis Mavromichalis   2C Ⓓ Gerren Lamson Ⓒ Cooke's Kitchen   2D Ⓓ Rudy Hurtado Global Branding Ⓒ Peter Costello

3A Ⓓ Rufuturu Ⓒ Consource   3B Ⓓ Ninet6 Ltd Ⓒ CIPHION   3C Ⓓ Traction Ⓒ CEMA   3D Ⓓ Bronson Ma Creative Ⓒ Cinnamon Perryman

4A Ⓓ BluesCue Designs Ⓒ BluesCue Designs   4B Ⓓ Schifino Lee Advertising Ⓒ Schifino Lee Advertising   4C Ⓓ Double O Design Ⓒ TRM Developments   4D Ⓓ eight a.m. brand design (shanghai) Co., Ltd Ⓒ C2 MEDICAL SPA

5A Ⓓ Gardner Design Ⓒ D Construction   5B Ⓓ Sebastiany Branding & Design Ⓒ Cuattro   5C Ⓓ Emilio Correa Ⓒ Double   5D Ⓓ Extrabrand Ⓒ Extrabrand

	A	B	C	D
1				

| designbureau

 doteo Polska

diane ingarten™

e-cycling

ED'S ELECTRIC

elineate

enormousfoot

ETCOPTICAL

French Bakery

FRONTIER FENCING STUDIO
NEW YORK

EB ARCH
PARTNERS

Ⓓ = Design Firm   Ⓒ = Client

1A Ⓓ RICH design studio Ⓒ Intellservice printhouse 1B Ⓓ alekchmura.com Ⓒ Alek Chmura 1C Ⓓ Depikt Ⓒ Delicious Coaching 1D Ⓓ Jenny Ng Ⓒ Dachis Group

2A Ⓓ alekchmura.com Ⓒ Alek Chmura 2B Ⓓ Bronson Ma Creative Ⓒ Execentus 2C Ⓓ Christopher Dina Ⓒ The 4th Bin (competition) 2D Ⓓ Siah Design Ⓒ Eds Electric

3A Ⓓ Range Ⓒ National Renewable Energy Laboratory 3B Ⓓ Roy Smith Design Ⓒ elineate 3C Ⓓ mIQelangelo Ⓒ Miroslav Vujovic 3D Ⓓ Hibblen Design Ⓒ Firestone

4A Ⓓ Logoholik Ⓒ Bojan Stefanovic 4B Ⓓ PUSH Branding and Design Ⓒ PUSH Branding and Design 4C Ⓓ bartodell.com Ⓒ East Valley Construction Incorporated 4D Ⓓ TypeOrange Ⓒ EB Arch + Partners

5A Ⓓ TRUF Ⓒ Evolvinx 5B Ⓓ Sakideamsheni Ⓒ Bread Bakery 5C Ⓓ oLo Brand group Ⓒ Frontier Fencing 5D Ⓓ Patten ID Ⓒ Shortfusegear.com

	A	B	C	D
1				
2				
3				
4	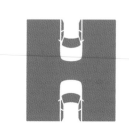			
5				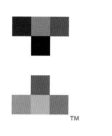

Ⓓ = Design Firm   Ⓒ = Client

1A Ⓓ Carrihan Creative Group Ⓒ FLIRT SALON   1B Ⓓ Pentagram Design Ⓒ Fort Worth Museum   1C Ⓓ Niedermeier Design Ⓒ First Fidelity   1D Ⓓ 3 Advertising LLC Ⓒ F8 Photography

2A Ⓓ Love Communications Ⓒ PerpetualGreen   2B Ⓓ Kristian Andersen + Associates Ⓒ Graphite   2C Ⓓ Gizwiz Studio Ⓒ Tee Yee Ping   2D Ⓓ Storeyville Ⓒ 919 Marketing for Glenveigh Pharmaceuticals

3A Ⓓ Mattson Creative Ⓒ p11 Creative   3B Ⓓ Indaco Ⓒ Galerie Gmurzynska   3C Ⓓ Pure Fusion Media Ⓒ Grace   3D Ⓓ entz creative Ⓒ Gateway 5

4A Ⓓ Fuller Ⓒ Hall Technical   4B Ⓓ Pavone Ⓒ Hallman Neighborhoods   4C Ⓓ TOKY Branding+Design Ⓒ Hanke Construction   4D Ⓓ Third Planet Communications Ⓒ Hause Distribution

5A Ⓓ H. Ⓒ Hache Creativos SCP   5B Ⓓ TunnelBravo Ⓒ Johnny Miller Golf   5C Ⓓ Kastelov Ⓒ Holden Group   5D Ⓓ bartodell.com Ⓒ Amarillo Hispanic Chamber of Commerce

A **B** **C** **D**

1

HEATON
ERECTORS INCORPORATED

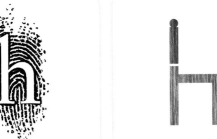

2

MICHAEL J. TOOLE DDS

3

 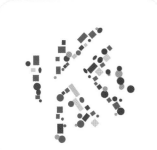  

4

5

Ⓓ = Design Firm   Ⓒ = Client

1A Ⓓ Dallas Duncan Design Ⓒ Heaton Erecting   1B Ⓓ Gavula Design Associates Ⓒ Hendrickson Photography   1C Ⓓ ivan_aran_design_studio Ⓒ i.n. Ivana Nikolish Interiors   1D Ⓓ Drink Red Creative Ⓒ Heather Benjamin Jewelry

2A Ⓓ CopperCoast Ⓒ iLove   2B Ⓓ Rock Creek Strategic Marketing Ⓒ iSymmetry   2C Ⓓ Chad Mjos Ⓒ Michael J. Toole DDS   2D Ⓓ Rudy Hurtado Global Branding Ⓒ Jazz School Online

3A Ⓓ Mahimoto Ⓒ Legofish   3B Ⓓ Smith & Jones Ⓒ Kieselstein Law Firm PLLC   3C Ⓓ KW43 BRANDDESIGN Ⓒ Kenstone   3D Ⓓ Sebastiany Branding & Design Ⓒ Keb

4A Ⓓ Bronson Ma Creative Ⓒ Kleckner Consulting   4B Ⓓ Studio International Ⓒ Kutina city   4C Ⓓ Traction Ⓒ Tumelo Group   4D Ⓓ Vlad Ermolaev Ⓒ KTO

5A Ⓓ Flight Deck Creative Ⓒ Legacy Maintenance   5B Ⓓ Porkka & Kuutsa Oy Ⓒ Leipurin Oy   5C Ⓓ Miller Creative LLC Ⓒ Lush Toffee   5D Ⓓ raudesign Ⓒ Dr. Karen La

1

2

3

4

5

ⓓ = Design Firm   ⓒ = Client

1A ⓓ Davina Chatkeon Design ⓒ mark walat 1B ⓓ Tran Creative ⓒ Madison Home 1C ⓓ Fernandez Design ⓒ Mendocino Vineyards 1D ⓓ Down With Design ⓒ 44 More

2A ⓓ creative space ⓒ Pat Wolf - museum momentum 2B ⓓ julian peck ⓒ Julian Peck 2C ⓓ Matador Design Studio ⓒ Matador Design Studio 2D ⓓ wierhouse ⓒ Magnolia Properties

3A ⓓ TOKY Branding+Design ⓒ Messiah Lutheran Church 3B ⓓ M. Brady Clark Design ⓒ Larry Miller & Co 3C ⓓ Marlin ⓒ Made 3D ⓓ Michael Spitz ⓒ Michael Spitz

4A ⓓ Deep See Design ⓒ Mecham Lawn Service 4B ⓓ JM Designs ⓒ Medialliance 4C ⓓ Chad Mjos ⓒ Moda Architecture 4D ⓓ alekchmura.com ⓒ Micasa

5A ⓓ Fernandez Design ⓒ Moore IT Services 5B ⓓ Brand Harvest Consultancy Pvt Ltd ⓒ NowPos Online Services Pvt. Ltd. 5C ⓓ NOMADESIGN Inc. ⓒ Mahoroba 5D ⓓ Helius Creative Advertising ⓒ Mike Bailey Printing

A	B	C	D	

Dr. med. Michael Bach
GASTROENTEROLOGE

CONSTRUCTORA S.A.S

 1

One Million Meals A Month

MARIA PRZYBYSZ
PHOTOGRAPHY

 2

LOGISTICA

M+YC

 3

NAWGAN 4

neehao

 5

ⓓ = Design Firm ⓒ = Client

1A ⓓ Josef Stapel ⓒ Michael bach 1B ⓓ Art Machine ⓒ MetalBrands 1C ⓓ Juancazu ⓒ Juan Carlos Zuluaga 1D ⓓ Lippincott ⓒ Meredith

2A ⓓ Webster Design Associates Inc. ⓒ Webster Design Associates Inc. 2B ⓓ SEMAFOR ⓒ Maria Przybysz 2C ⓓ bartodell.com ⓒ Jamie Roche 2D ⓓ Headwerk ⓒ Material Witness

3A ⓓ www.n1kk3l.com ⓒ MW Logistica 3B ⓓ Axygene ⓒ Virtual World of Music / NDI Media 3C ⓓ Axygene ⓒ Me & You Clothing 3D ⓓ Visual Unity ⓒ Made 2 Order

4A ⓓ Bozell ⓒ North Star Foundation 4B ⓓ William Herod Design ⓒ Open Door Neighbor 4C ⓓ The Drawing Board ⓒ Navitus Media 4D ⓓ Propaganda Inc. ⓒ Nawgan

5A ⓓ RetroMetro Designs ⓒ neehao language schools 5B ⓓ Glitschka Studios ⓒ New Modern Science 5C ⓓ SparrowDesign ⓒ WiedzaNet 5D ⓓ Transformer Studio ⓒ Media Alliance JSC

	A	B	C	D
1				
2				
3				
4				
5				

D = Design Firm   C = Client

1A D Webster Design Associates Inc. C Omaha Public Library   1B D Archrival C Nomad Lounge   1C D A.D. Creative Group C Off The Leaf   1D D Spring Advertising + Design C Nuovo

2A D Design Practice, Inc. C Rieches/Baird Advertising   2B D Studio Ink C OpenCandy   2C D Stoller Design Group C Office of Matthew Gaber   2D D Firefly Branding Boutique C Tandem Consulting

3A D Rise Design Branding Inc. C Powerful Industry Corporation   3B D Kuznetsov Evgeniy | KUZNETS C Region Protsessing   3C D Kuznetsov Evgeniy | KUZNETS C Region Protsessing   3D D idApostle C idApostle

4A D Jon Briggs Design C Patricia Stewart   4B D Kolar Advertising and Marketing C Michael Pratt   4C D Six17 C Pacific Shore Capital   4D D Indicia Design Inc C Phenix

5A D Tomasz Politanski Design C Tomasz Politanski   5B D Ehlinger C Pylant   5C D Gizwiz Studio C Esther   5D D 28 LIMITED BRAND C Probierzähne

78

A	B	C	D	
				1
				2
				3
				4
				5

Ⓓ = Design Firm   Ⓒ = Client

1A Ⓓ Colin Saito Ⓒ C&D Zodiac   1B Ⓓ Paraphernalia Design Ⓒ Film Australia   1C Ⓓ bartodell.com Ⓒ Threeleaf.tv   1D Ⓓ Anthony Lane Studios Ⓒ Paris Holley

2A Ⓓ Gizwiz Studio Ⓒ Tee Yee Ping   2B Ⓓ Communication Agency Ⓒ Pavel Surovy   2C Ⓓ Fargo Design Co., Inc. Ⓒ Shadyside Academy   2D Ⓓ Latinbrand Ⓒ La Quinta

3A Ⓓ IF marketing & advertising Ⓒ Shawn Ng   3B Ⓓ Chris Rooney Illustration/Design Ⓒ Ramsell   3C Ⓓ R&R Partners Ⓒ Honolulu Transit   3D Ⓓ Rickabaugh Graphics Ⓒ Rollins College

4A Ⓓ Able Ⓒ Redeemer Presbyterian Church   4B Ⓓ Brent Couchman Design Ⓒ Rosalyn Perry   4C Ⓓ Hayes Image Ⓒ Roberto Bertelli Furniture   4D Ⓓ Special Modern Design Ⓒ LAB Collaborative

5A Ⓓ Naughtyfish Ⓒ Edwards Dunlop papers   5B Ⓓ Schwartzrock Graphic Arts Ⓒ Design Center   5C Ⓓ KONIAK DESIGN Ⓒ Rhus Ovata fashion brand   5D Ⓓ Schwartzrock Graphic Arts Ⓒ Design Center

	A	B	C	D
1				
2				
3				
4				
5				

Ⓓ = Design Firm   Ⓒ = Client

1A Ⓓ TEDDYSHIPLEY Ⓒ CashCow Services   1B Ⓓ SANDIA, Inc. Ⓒ Securics   1C Ⓓ Denis Olenik Design Studio Ⓒ Denis Olenik   1D Ⓓ Indicia Design Inc Ⓒ Saints Pub + Patio

2A Ⓓ Michael Spitz Ⓒ Michael Spitz   2B Ⓓ Logoholik Ⓒ SourcingFactory.com   2C Ⓓ Essex Two Ⓒ City of Sunset Beach   2D Ⓓ TAMER KOSELI Ⓒ Sakarya University Energy Technologies Team

3A Ⓓ Denis Olenik Design Studio Ⓒ Avivo   3B Ⓓ Dalius Stuoka Ⓒ Stairs   3C Ⓓ Karl Design Vienna Ⓒ Seydler AG Frankfurt   3D Ⓓ Lemon Design Pvt Ltd Ⓒ Stratel India

4A Ⓓ Banowetz + Company, Inc. Ⓒ Stephan Pyles   4B Ⓓ KITA International | Visual Playground Ⓒ skischule mittberg   4C Ⓓ Deep See Design Ⓒ Geri G Cosmetics   4D Ⓓ Klundt Hosmer Ⓒ Second Nature Wilderness Programs

5A Ⓓ Niedermeier Design Ⓒ slipstream   5B Ⓓ Kreativer Kopf Ⓒ Schoen und Wider Druck   5C Ⓓ Almosh82 Ⓒ Almosh82   5D Ⓓ Gerren Lamson Ⓒ Thayer Upholstery

TOLLEFSON PLAZA

TITANIUM
SOLUTIONS

TYRRELL
DESIGN

TELKO

1

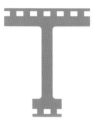

2

UNIBOX

UNION ASPECT

3

HOUSE OF VAYNE

vertika

4

WISCH
MEDIA

fashionworks

5

ⓓ = Design Firm   ⓒ = Client

1A ⓓ Rusty George Creative ⓒ Chamber of Commerce   1B ⓓ max2o ⓒ Titanium Solutions   1C ⓓ Richard Baird Ltd ⓒ Richard Baird   1D ⓓ Porkka & Kuutsa Oy ⓒ Telko Oy

2A ⓓ Down With Design ⓒ Theo's Cycle Shop   2B ⓓ Down With Design ⓒ Techton   2C ⓓ Flight Deck Creative ⓒ Robert Tullier   2D ⓓ Dalius Stuoka ⓒ Dalius Stuoka

3A ⓓ UlrichPinciotti Design Group ⓒ University of Toledo   3B ⓓ BrandLab Moscow ⓒ BrandLab Moscow   3C ⓓ Logoholik ⓒ Bojan Stefanovic   3D ⓓ Just Creative Design ⓒ Vero

4A ⓓ R&R Partners ⓒ Busch Entertainment/Busch Gardens Tampa Bay   4B ⓓ KROG, d.o.o. ⓒ Slovenska knjiga   4C ⓓ Lemon Design Pvt Ltd ⓒ Rafee Media Group   4D ⓓ Oxide Design Co. ⓒ Quantum Workplace

5A ⓓ markosoti.com ⓒ Emil Wisch   5B ⓓ Wibye Advertising & Graphic Design ⓒ Fashionworks   5C ⓓ izm ⓒ Willow Road   5D ⓓ Flash Bang ⓒ Webfilings

	A	B	C	D
1				
2				
3				...

Ⓓ = Design Firm　Ⓒ = Client

1A Ⓓ lis design Ⓒ Elisa Sheehan　1B Ⓓ NOT A CANNED HAM Ⓒ Water Solutions　1C Ⓓ Neworld Associates Ⓒ The National Wax Museum　1D Ⓓ wray ward Ⓒ Woolpert

2A Ⓓ blacksheepdesign Ⓒ Wolcan Construction　2B Ⓓ Fierce Competitors Ⓒ Paul Wronski　2C Ⓓ Gardner Design Ⓒ Wichita State University　2D Ⓓ julian peck Ⓒ Julian Peck

3A Ⓓ Altagraf Ⓒ AstraZeneca　3B Ⓓ Range Ⓒ Xchange Technologies　3C Ⓓ Judson Design Ⓒ Amerex Energy services　3D Ⓓ diffuse.ru Ⓒ Russian Idea

4A Ⓓ Sebastiany Branding & Design Ⓒ Transdata　4B Ⓓ Banowetz + Company, Inc. Ⓒ Tim Sutton　4C Ⓓ Roy Smith Design Ⓒ World Moto　4D Ⓓ Anna Kovecses Ⓒ zapphire

5A Ⓓ Wizemark Ⓒ Zeugma　5B Ⓓ Today Ⓒ Nelson　5C Ⓓ jamjardesign Ⓒ ZINZIN　5D Ⓓ RICH design studio Ⓒ Zoom Creative Studio

	A	B	C	D	
	 zerojeden	 Spins	 THIRD STREET CENTER		1
		 mrkt.7			2
	 VANITY 9		4⁹	 apteka69.pl	3
			360°		4
	 555 BARTLETT	 ONE MILLION MEALS A MONTH			5

(D) = Design Firm   (C) = Client

1A (D) Jarek Kowalczyk (C) Jarek Kowalczyk 1B (D) Anna Kovecses (C) 3Spins 1C (D) rainy day designs (C) Third Street Center 1D (D) Neworld Associates (C) 4fm

2A (D) M. Brady Clark Design (C) gomerch 2B (D) Steven O'Connor (C) Turner Associates 2C (D) Gizwiz Studio (C) Chuah Shue Ping 2D (D) Deep See Design (C) Cloud Nine Travel Accesories

3A (D) RICH design studio (C) Vanity Nine 3B (D) Colin Saito (C) C&D Zodiac 3C (D) Glacier (C) Arteis 3D (D) alekchmura.com (C) Alek Chmura

4A (D) Betterweather (C) Avery Dennison Corporate Communications 4B (D) Go Welsh (C) Penn State Architecture 4C (D) DTM_INC (C) Vodafone 4D (D) Partners + Napier (C) 360 | 365 Film Festival

5A (D) Mattson Creative (C) p11 Creative 5B (D) Webster Design Associates Inc. (C) Webster Design Associates Inc. 5C (D) Arispe Creative (C) Font Aid IV 5D (D) Anna Kovecses (C) mottoviva

Garden Club of Irvington-on-Hudson
Identity Design

Visual Language LLC, Irvington, New York

A grand event in a grand setting deserves a grand identity. Ellen Shapiro of Visual Language LLC had the event, the setting, and the opportunity to create an identity and logo to match.

In April 2010, the Garden Club of Irvington-on-Hudson held a Garden Club of America flower show, its first in more than a decade. That meant it was organized and judged according to rigorous standards set by GCA, a national organization dedicated to artistic and horticultural excellence, conservation, and civic improvement. The show was held in the carriage house of Lyndhurst, a National Trust Historic Site, whose Gothic-style mansion overlooking the Hudson River in Tarrytown, New York, was home to railroad tycoon Jay Gould and his family.

In 1881, the Goulds built a magnificent glass greenhouse on Lyndhurst's grounds, where a staff of gardeners raised plants and flowers for the family's lavish entertaining. The Irvington Club's show was called "The Gilded Cage" (a play on a common reference to the Victorian or "gilded age"). The show celebrated Lyndhurst through displays of Victorian-style flower arrangements and horticultural specimens including orchids, ferns, and branches of local trees in bloom. But it was definitely a modern event, visited over three days by hundreds of local citizens and gardening aficionados.

The show needed a logo that would inspire people to attend by communicating the show's theme and the architectural style of Lyndhurst. "I usually explore a number of different concepts when designing a logo," says Shapiro, "but I had a specific idea in mind for this, which was to capture the spirit and shape of the greenhouse, as if its Gothic arches were rendered in one continuous fine line, like Spencerian calligraphy."

The resultant logo's intricate patterning intrigues the brain and directs the eye upward. Although it may look like calligraphy, the logo is actually a repeat pattern of an arch drawn in Adobe Illustrator

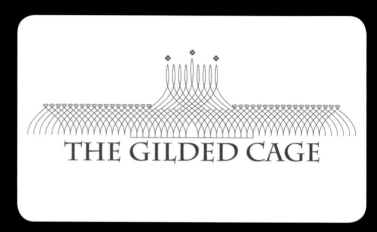

The Gilded Cage logo, created by Visual Language LLC, appears delicate, but holds up well even on a complicated background.

by Shapiro's assistant, designer Emily Shields, following a sketch Shapiro did from photographs they took at the greenhouse.

The logo typeface, Charlemagne Standard Bold, says Shapiro, is one of those fonts that come with the Mac OS or Adobe Creative Suite. "I usually eschew them in favor of typefaces purchased specifically for client projects, but the rounded letterforms and pointy serifs just seemed right for this."

Because it was a pro bono project, Shapiro's team was challenged to produce the signage, program, invitations, fliers, and other collateral at very low cost. The visuals are a combination of stock images of roses, historic photographs from Lyndhurst's collection, engravings of flowers from Dover CDs, and photographs shot by Shapiro and Shields. For the invitation and other key applications, the logo was rendered in gold ("CMYK, not gold foil stamping") on an iStock photo background of red roses. The success of these efforts was proven out by the enthusiastic response by Garden Club members and visitors to the show, as well as the awarding of a special commendation by the Garden Club of America.

LOGO SEARCH

Keywords **Typography**

Type: ○ Symbol ○ Typographic ○ Combo ● All

	A	B	C	D

1 — cafe /® · **S7n city**

2 — pr*tty sh*tty · ignite · Creative english · Berta Medina ['berta meðina] english teacher

3 — cigaru · mon♡gamy · St. Maur · MATADOR

4 — DRACULA · 3OPERA! 1979-2009 · EARTHTECH · TICKETS.COM

5 — JUSar Kancelaria Prawa Podatkowego Jaroslaw Ursyn-Szantyr Julita Ursyn-Szantyr · HONOR of COWBOYS CATTLE BARON'S BALL 2009 · VERVE COFFEE ROASTERS · INVERNIS

Ⓓ = Design Firm   Ⓒ = Client

1C Ⓓ Nadim Twal Ⓒ Mass Awarness   1D Ⓓ H2 Design of Texas Ⓒ Las Vegas

2A Ⓓ Josh Berta Ⓒ prttyshtty.com   2B Ⓓ AkinsParker Creative Ⓒ Ignite Creative Solutions   2C Ⓓ Zieldesign Ⓒ Creativ English   2D Ⓓ El Paso, Galeria de Comunicacion Ⓒ Berta Medina

3A Ⓓ VINNA KARTIKA design Ⓒ Cigaru Gold Mining   3B Ⓓ CF Napa Brand Design Ⓒ Canopy Management   3C Ⓓ see+co Ⓒ St. Maur Estate Wines   3D Ⓓ concussion, llc Ⓒ Matador

4A Ⓓ Flight Deck Creative Ⓒ David Beck   4B Ⓓ Dallas Duncan Design Ⓒ Dallas Duncan Franklin   4C Ⓓ Ehlinger Ⓒ Chad Ehlinger   4D Ⓓ Tom Hughes Ⓒ Tickets.com / Idealab

5A Ⓓ MP Design Ⓒ Law Offices of Jaroslaw Ursyn-Szantyr and Julita Ursyn-Szantyr   5B Ⓓ ChapmanCreative Ⓒ Dallas Cattle Baron's Ball   5C Ⓓ Chen Design Associates Ⓒ Verve Coffee Roasters   5D Ⓓ Logoholik Ⓒ Bojan Stefanovic

	A	B	C	D
1	maxa	ogol	go smart	Trava
2	k._lled PRODUCTIONS	Dr.Bruce Glazzzzer	novella	truce
3	thought faqtory	communic8	speak PR	talk
4	engage! 	elope	back	dot com factory 
5	pencil	Fireworks	benchfed	PlayGround

Ⓓ = Design Firm　Ⓒ = Client

1A Ⓓ alekchmura.com Ⓒ Alek Chmura　1B Ⓓ Anna Kovecses Ⓒ ogol　1C Ⓓ Fleishman Hillard Ⓒ National Head Start Association　1D Ⓓ Dalius Stuoka Ⓒ Trava

2A Ⓓ Sean Heisler Ⓒ Sean Heisler　2B Ⓓ Ceb Design Ⓒ Dr. Bruce Glazer　2C Ⓓ Motto Ⓒ Novella Books　2D Ⓓ Turner Duckworth Ⓒ Refreshment Brands

3A Ⓓ CopperCoast Ⓒ Thought Faqtory　3B Ⓓ Sky High Advertising FZ LLC Ⓒ Communic8　3C Ⓓ PUSH Branding and Design Ⓒ Speak　3D Ⓓ Karl Design Vienna Ⓒ Karl Design Vienna

4A Ⓓ Brand Innovation Group Ⓒ Ambassador Family Enterprises　4B Ⓓ julian peck Ⓒ Sarah Chang　4C Ⓓ milou Ⓒ back　4D Ⓓ GUIPON M.D.S. Ⓒ Dot Com Factory

5A Ⓓ Reghardt Ⓒ Reghardt Grobbelaar　5B Ⓓ The Key Ⓒ Studio Fireworks　5C Ⓓ Matchstic Ⓒ Gift Card Giver　5D Ⓓ entz creative Ⓒ Denis Wong

	A	B	C	D
1	50bar	seedmoney	canoodle PASTA COMPANY	incrediblebank℠
2	switch	misread	spoiled	pango
3	formspring	United	redwave SYSTEMS	ecoxera
4	dos puntos	Ojo Optometry	BlackBerry™	Walmart
5	adidas RUN FOR THEIR LIVES!	(F$_o$)Rm$_u$La	METRIC	theobroma CHOCOLATE LOUNGE

Ⓓ = Design Firm Ⓒ = Client

1A Ⓓ Karl Design Vienna Ⓒ 50bar Tauch GmbH 1B Ⓓ X3 Studios Ⓒ Seed Fund Management 1C Ⓓ Propaganda Inc. Ⓒ Metromedia Restaurant Group 1D Ⓓ jonskaggs.com Ⓒ Incredible Bank

2A Ⓓ Campbell Fisher Design Ⓒ bda Sports 2B Ⓓ pricedyment Ⓒ misread 2C Ⓓ Spring Advertising + Design Ⓒ Spoiled 2D Ⓓ XY ARTS Ⓒ Pango

3A Ⓓ Kristian Andersen + Associates Ⓒ FormSpring 3B Ⓓ Ferreira Design Company Ⓒ United Capital Financial 3C Ⓓ Just Creative Design Ⓒ Redwave Systems 3D Ⓓ SGNL Studio Ⓒ Ecoxera

4A Ⓓ Romulo Moya / Trama Ⓒ Centro Literario dos puntos 4B Ⓓ SignalSmith Design Ⓒ Ojo Oprometry 4C Ⓓ Landor Associates Ⓒ BlackBerry 4D Ⓓ Lippincott Ⓒ Walmart

5A Ⓓ Karl Design Vienna Ⓒ Karl Design / Proposal for a charity run against aids 5B Ⓓ Sakideamsheni Ⓒ george Bokhua 5C Ⓓ Indicia Design Inc Ⓒ Indicia Design Inc 5D Ⓓ Imagine Creative Ⓒ Theobroma Chocolate Lounge

	A	B	C	D
1	AVIO	COCOON	SNAP	SMYLO 
2	CLOUD	PORK	PING 	PONZU SUSHI HOUSE
3	GESUNDE WOHNKULTUR KROOSS	YÖDA CODA	EYE LEVEL ART	MY DAILY PIC
4	HOME ON HOWE	OPEN DOOR reality show	COFFEE CSA.ORG · SUBSCRIBE TO FAMILY FARMS	VON FR/ EDR \CH 
5	EDGE	RAW	PODIUM	FOCUS™

Ⓓ = Design Firm   Ⓒ = Client

1A Ⓓ Aroosha Design Ⓒ AVIO 1B Ⓓ MDM Design Ⓒ Cocoon Bar 1C Ⓓ Sakideamsheni Ⓒ George Bokhua 1D Ⓓ Andrei D. Popa Ⓒ Smylo

2A Ⓓ Kastelov Ⓒ Richard Cloud 2B Ⓓ Splash:Design Ⓒ Phred Martin and Moris Antosh 2C Ⓓ The Jake Group, LLC Ⓒ Veronique Morrison 2D Ⓓ Keo Pierron Ⓒ Ponzu Sushi House

3A Ⓓ Braue: Brand Design Experts Ⓒ Krooss - gesunde Wohnkultur 3B Ⓓ Cuie&Co Ⓒ Yoda Coda 3C Ⓓ HOOK Ⓒ Eye Level Art 3D Ⓓ Luxecetera, Inc. Ⓒ Ashley Jankowski

4A Ⓓ Spring Advertising + Design Ⓒ Urban Barn 4B Ⓓ mIQelangelo Ⓒ RTS 4C Ⓓ FUEL Creative Group Ⓒ CoffeeCSA.org 4D Ⓓ Martin Jordan Ⓒ University of Applied Sciences Potsdam

5A Ⓓ Ryan Russell Design Ⓒ Edge Advantage 5B Ⓓ Ishan Khosla Design Ⓒ Reaction Against War 5C Ⓓ concussion, llc Ⓒ Konami 5D Ⓓ visuALchemy Ⓒ Rohi Ch.

	A	B	C	D	

A **B** **C** **D**

MINORiTY RECRUiT	N XTMOVe	ENTERIOR	MENT_L BL_NK	1
EXHALE	SIX8 MEDIA	EIGHT	NYNE	2
HYPOHELP einfach finanzieren lassen	ОПТИМА	EXITIVE	CITIZEN PEOPLE + BRANDS + CULTURE	3
NIVEN LANDSCAPING	SEE - SAW	HOPE & ANCHOR	DØRRANCE PLANETARIUM	4
FLUENCE	GROUNDWORK	DEPAJ ديبج	قصر الدين	5

Ⓓ = Design Firm   Ⓒ = Client

1A Ⓓ Green Ink Studio Ⓒ Minority Recruit   1B Ⓓ Tom Hughes Ⓒ Next Move   1C Ⓓ CINDERBLOC CREATIVE Ⓒ CINDERBLOC   1D Ⓓ Benedict Sato Design Ⓒ Mental Blank

2A Ⓓ Extralarge, A Design Studio Ⓒ Exhale Therapeutics   2B Ⓓ TRK Studio Ⓒ SIX8 Media   2C Ⓓ 5Seven Ⓒ people against california prop 8   2D Ⓓ David Gramblin Ⓒ David Gramblin

3A Ⓓ Troyca - Visual Solutions GmbH Ⓒ Hypohelp   3B Ⓓ Extrabrand Ⓒ Adv Optima   3C Ⓓ Logoholik Ⓒ Bojan Stefanovic   3D Ⓓ Brian Haselton Ⓒ Citizen

4A Ⓓ Hayes Image Ⓒ Niven Landscaping   4B Ⓓ Down With Design Ⓒ www.see-saw.net   4C Ⓓ VIVA Creative Group Ⓒ Hope & Anchor   4D Ⓓ Worth | Design Ⓒ Arizona Science Center

5A Ⓓ Lemon Design Pvt Ltd Ⓒ Infologics   5B Ⓓ NOT A CANNED HAM Ⓒ BBDO Atlanta   5C Ⓓ Boxon Vision Ⓒ Depaj   5D Ⓓ Ghiath Lahham Ⓒ SOUTHERN SUN DUBAI

Cinereach
Identity Redesign

Method

Cinereach, a nonprofit film production company and foundation, was started by young philanthropists and filmmakers as a vehicle for promoting, funding, supporting, and producing well-crafted films that represent fresh and thought-provoking viewpoints. As the group's mission statement says, their goal is to champion "vital stories, artfully told."

The organization helps filmmakers in three specific ways: through its Reach Film Fellowship, a specialized program for early-career film-makers who are making socially conscious short films; Cinereach Productions, which searches for the stories behind the headlines, providing a new, personal take on national and international affairs; and Grants and Awards, which supports films that possess an inde-pendent spirit, depict underrepresented perspectives, and resonate across international boundaries.

The company's mission and values were not reflected properly in Cinereach's previous identity. Based on the concept of passport stamps, it spoke well to the idea of travel and the exploration of new cultures and ideas, but did not communicate the importance of craft and art in filmmaking or the multiple people and per-spectives that come together to tell a story through this medium. Another challenging aspect of the identity was that each of the company's three programs had its own unique stamp design that, when brought together with the Cinereach mark, created visual dissonance and an unclear brand hierarchy.

Cinereach approached Method (San Francisco, New York, and London) for help in refitting its identity. Milena Sadée, Method's design director, says that understanding *what* their client did was simple. Conveying the many different facets of their organization and vision of the company was more of a challenge.

"Creating films requires a convergence of people, resources, and ideas," she says. "The goal is to challenge people and expose them to these different stories and views so that hopefully a dia-logue is started and maybe even some prejudices challenged."

The new Cinereach identity, played out on business cards.

Although the designers were creating a new identity, the team real-ized there was still equity in the old mark. They looked at the red circle that was part of the core brand in the previous "stamped" identity and realized that by breaking it up and putting it back together, they could convey the notions of perspective and conver-gence. "We call the new mark 'the prism,'" says Sadée. "It speaks to the previous logo yet goes in a completely new direction."

While the core mark had been established, the identity still needed to be extended to Cinereach's three divisions. Narguess Noshirvani, senior program manager, explains that creating a sepa-rate mark for each of these areas could result in a similar brand hierarchy confusion that the company was already struggling with.

"We decided that color would be the most effective way to pro-duce a clear distinction among the three program areas and still communicate their connection to Cinereach and each other. We created three different color palettes that borrow from and build off of one another. Grants and Awards has a greenish-yellow to greenish-blue palette; the Reach Film Fellowship area has a palette that ranges from blues to pinks to purples; Productions ranges from oranges to reds."

LOGO SEARCH

Keywords | Enclosures

Type: ○ Symbol ○ Typographic ○ Combo ● All

1

2

3

4

5

Ⓓ = Design Firm   Ⓒ = Client

1C Ⓓ M. Brady Clark Design Ⓒ gomerch 1D Ⓓ Sakideamsheni Ⓒ Imedi TV

2A Ⓓ Filip Komorowski Ⓒ Filip Komorowski 2B Ⓓ Tweet Design Ⓒ Tweet Design 2C Ⓓ Tweet Design Ⓒ Full Service Music 2D Ⓓ Scott Oeschger Ⓒ M&M

3A Ⓓ The Brand Hatchery Ⓒ Three Blind Ants 3B Ⓓ Pop Ovidiu Sebastian Ⓒ Nige impex 3C Ⓓ The Jake Group, LLC Ⓒ Veronique Morrison 3D Ⓓ Hernandez Design Studio Ⓒ Jugar Creative

4A Ⓓ Stefan Romanu Ⓒ Allnet Telecom 4B Ⓓ SOULSEVEN Ⓒ True O2 4C Ⓓ iHua Design Ⓒ O.L. Style 4D Ⓓ a. pounds design Ⓒ Carol Chapman

5A Ⓓ AkarStudios Ⓒ Fresh Cutt 5B Ⓓ www.MikeyBurton.com Ⓒ 20x200 / Jen Bekman 5C Ⓓ Webster Design Associates Inc. Ⓒ Jones Bros. Cupcakes 5D Ⓓ Banowetz + Company, Inc. Ⓒ Tim McEneny

	A	B	C	D
1				
2				
3				
4				
5				

Ⓓ = Design Firm   Ⓒ = Client

1A Ⓓ Extrabrand Ⓒ Intesys   1B Ⓓ D&Dre Design Ⓒ Radiant   1C Ⓓ AT PACE Ⓒ Occhiali   1D Ⓓ Brent Couchman Design Ⓒ Tactik Interactive

2A Ⓓ Bailey Lauerman Ⓒ Nebraska Health and Human Services   2B Ⓓ Rose Ⓒ MFI & Lloyds TSB   2C Ⓓ Hilary Dana Williams Ⓒ atitu   2D Ⓓ rajasandhu.com Ⓒ Ikon

3A Ⓓ ARTENTIKO Ⓒ PSO Sp. z.o.o   3B Ⓓ Jesse Kirsch Ⓒ Melt Chocolate   3C Ⓓ Holler Design Ⓒ Rojo Architecture   3D Ⓓ Romulo Moya / Trama Ⓒ Colegio de Arquitectos del Ecuador

4A Ⓓ PUSH Branding and Design Ⓒ Blur MediaWorks   4B Ⓓ raudesign Ⓒ Double Dragon Chinese Restaurant   4C Ⓓ Lucero Design Ⓒ Calle 66   4D Ⓓ eleven07 Ⓒ Tijuana Gift Shop

5A Ⓓ orangebird Ⓒ take 3 studios   5B Ⓓ LogoDesignGuru.com Ⓒ Tajdar Sultan   5C Ⓓ eight a.m. brand design (shanghai) Co., Ltd Ⓒ WWW.8-A-M.COM   5D Ⓓ Kevin Zwirble Design Co. Ⓒ Paul Minor Band

A	B	C	D	
				1
				2
				3
				4
				5

Ⓓ = Design Firm   Ⓒ = Client

1A Ⓓ Muhina Design Ⓒ KIAF   1B Ⓓ The Navicor Group Ⓒ Susan Albert   1C Ⓓ nelnet Ⓒ WikiDebate   1D Ⓓ Kommunikat Ⓒ Jakub Rutkowski

2A Ⓓ The Pink Pear Design Company Ⓒ Bi-State Autism Initiative (proposed)   2B Ⓓ LindyLazar Marketing Ⓒ Annie's of Traverse City   2C Ⓓ Glitschka Studios Ⓒ Veer   2D Ⓓ adamgf Ⓒ frut smoothies

3A Ⓓ Ishan Khosla Design Ⓒ Jaipur Virasat Foundation and Anantaya   3B Ⓓ Sockeye Creative Ⓒ Travel Portland   3C Ⓓ Brotbeck Corporate Design AG Ⓒ BIHAG Bieler Holzbau AG

3D Ⓓ Hazen Creative, Inc. Ⓒ EPIC - Engaging Philanthropy   4A Ⓓ Oxide Design Co. Ⓒ The Biatomic Point   4B Ⓓ Sudduth Design Co. Ⓒ Hill Country Scouts   4C Ⓓ PUSH Branding and Design Ⓒ CMMI Marketplace

4D Ⓓ DEI Creative Ⓒ GTS Development   5A Ⓓ Tomko Design Ⓒ PURO Gelato   5B Ⓓ Schwartzrock Graphic Arts Ⓒ BI   5C Ⓓ Rock Creek Strategic Marketing Ⓒ Pitango Gelato   5D Ⓓ Banowetz + Company, Inc. Ⓒ Kent Rathbun

	A	B	C	D
1				
2				
3				
4				
5				

Ⓓ = Design Firm   Ⓒ = Client

1A Ⓓ Sudduth Design Co. Ⓒ Lush Landscape Design   1B Ⓓ Kilmer & Kilmer Ⓒ Albuquerque Youth Symphony   1C Ⓓ Tweet Design Ⓒ Covet   1D Ⓓ Robin Easter Design Ⓒ Pumps: A Shoe Boutique

2A Ⓓ University of North Texas Ⓒ University of North Texas   2B Ⓓ Majorminor Ⓒ Cumulous   2C Ⓓ 1981 Ⓒ 1981   2D Ⓓ Artini Bar Designs Ⓒ spec

3A Ⓓ Rovillo Design Associates Ⓒ Harding Road   3B Ⓓ Ferreira Design Company Ⓒ Coca-Cola Mexico   3C Ⓓ Stuph Clothing Ⓒ Love At War   3D Ⓓ Double A Creative Ⓒ Makeup By Amber

4A Ⓓ SOULSEVEN Ⓒ Target - MoMA   4B Ⓓ Spoonbend Ⓒ Obrien Architecture   4C Ⓓ Stitch Design Co. Ⓒ The James Pond   4D Ⓓ Cricket Design Works Ⓒ Forward Music Festival

5A Ⓓ Periscope Ⓒ Michelle Rollins   5B Ⓓ Strange Ideas Ⓒ James Strange   5C Ⓓ Chris Trivizas | Design Ⓒ Zisimopoulou Stamatia   5D Ⓓ Timber Design Company Ⓒ Hancock Regional Hospital

LOGO SEARCH

Keywords **Display Type**

Type: ◯ Symbol ◯ Typographic ◯ Combo ⦿ All

A B C D

1

2

3

4

5

ⓓ = Design Firm   ⓒ = Client

1C ⓓ Filip Komorowski ⓒ Spy Club   1D ⓓ Glitschka Studios ⓒ Beloved Virus

2A ⓓ Hai Truong ⓒ The Asian Night Group   2B ⓓ Evoke International Design ⓒ Boutique Empire   2C ⓓ Limon Agencia Creativa ⓒ Front Desing Agency y el Gobierno de Playa del Carmen   2D ⓓ Farm Design ⓒ 10 Squared

3A ⓓ Glitschka Studios ⓒ Sinestra Fencing Team   3B ⓓ Caliber Creative, LLC ⓒ D'Vine Wine   3C ⓓ Stuph Clothing ⓒ Harris III Master Illusionist   3D ⓓ Moss Creative ⓒ The Ghazi Company

4A ⓓ Scott Oeschger ⓒ The Star Group   4B ⓓ DTM_INC ⓒ Chocxx   4C ⓓ Karl Design Vienna ⓒ Karl Design / Trendworxx   4D ⓓ Stuph Clothing ⓒ Stuph Clothing

5A ⓓ Turner Duckworth ⓒ Metallica   5B ⓓ Schwartzrock Graphic Arts ⓒ Sherwin Schwartzrock   5C ⓓ Razor Creative ⓒ New Brunswick Youth Orchestra   5D ⓓ ADC Global Creativity ⓒ Lake Arrowhead Community Services District

	A	B	C	D
1	FreeSpeak		Wad.R.T	
2	SWEET Little THINGS	Alcoholic Sunrise	GROOVY SPOON	POPeYeS
3	TERMINAL	THE LITTLE RED WAGON DAYCARE	BRAT BRATU	HAPPY HALLOWEEN FROM tommaso.inc
4	JULIAN PECK SAMPLE WORK 2006	FYLA	5IRE!	DEN
5	GEDENK	The LARKINS	DES MOINES PLAYHOUSE	Explorer Guide SCAVENGER HUNT

Ⓓ = Design Firm Ⓒ = Client

1A Ⓓ rowland design & art direction Ⓒ Fultz Marketing 1B Ⓓ Brent Couchman Design Ⓒ Heartbeat Clothing 1C Ⓓ diffuse.ru Ⓒ Dirt Wader 1D Ⓓ Black Bridge Ⓒ Community Recordings

2A Ⓓ Naughtyfish Ⓒ Sweet Little Things 2B Ⓓ THE LIVING CONSPIRACY Ⓒ Alcoholic Sunrise 2C Ⓓ IF marketing & advertising Ⓒ groovy spoon 2D Ⓓ Pentagram Design Ⓒ Popeyes

3A Ⓓ Armada d. o. o. Ⓒ F. S. L. d. o. o. 3B Ⓓ Chris Rooney Illustration/Design Ⓒ The Little Red Wagon Daycare 3C Ⓓ Armada d. o. o. Ⓒ Glocorb services Ltd. 3D Ⓓ origo branding company Ⓒ Tommaso Inc.

4A Ⓓ julian peck Ⓒ Julian Peck 4B Ⓓ The Drawing Board Ⓒ Florida Church of God 4C Ⓓ A3 Design Ⓒ Rochester Fire Dept. 4D Ⓓ Daniel Fernandez Ⓒ Marriott Vacation Club

5A Ⓓ Empax Ⓒ Gedenk 5B Ⓓ eleven07 Ⓒ Audium Entertainment 5C Ⓓ Cooper Smith and Company Ⓒ Des Moines Playhouse 5D Ⓓ Lunar Cow Ⓒ Six Flags Discovery Kingdom

A	**B**	**C**	**D**	
				1
				2
				3
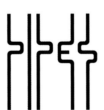				4
				5

ivy

Ⓓ = Design Firm   Ⓒ = Client

1A Ⓓ BrandBerry Ⓒ Pixo 1B Ⓓ Chris Rooney Illustration/Design Ⓒ Vyyo 1C Ⓓ TAMER KOSELI Ⓒ fizy 1D Ⓓ Indelible Ⓒ Michael

2A Ⓓ julian peck Ⓒ Sea Change 2B Ⓓ oLo Brand group Ⓒ Peeq Media 2C Ⓓ Britt Funderburk Ⓒ Britt Funderburk 2D Ⓓ rajasandhu.com Ⓒ Raja Sandhu

3A Ⓓ Interrobang Design Collaborative, Inc. Ⓒ zero2sixty creative 3B Ⓓ LeBoYe Ⓒ Forum Digital Graphic Forum 3C Ⓓ Communication Agency Ⓒ MOBIMAG 3D Ⓓ Maycreate Ⓒ On Point

4A Ⓓ R&R Partners Ⓒ Las Vegas Convention & Visitors Authority 4B Ⓓ GeniusLogo Ⓒ pipes 4C Ⓓ Yotam Hadar Ⓒ Flow 4D Ⓓ Almosh82 Ⓒ almosh82

5A Ⓓ mIQelangelo Ⓒ Ivy 5B Ⓓ Dalius Stuoka Ⓒ Dalius Stuoka 5C Ⓓ D&i (Design and Image) Ⓒ [DOCA] Denver office of Cultural Affairs 5D Ⓓ Karl Design Vienna Ⓒ Karl Design Vienna

	A	B	C	D
1				
2				
3				
4				
5				

Ⓓ = Design Firm   Ⓒ = Client

1A Ⓓ Ph.D Ⓒ Ciudad   1B Ⓓ Luxecetera, Inc. Ⓒ Ashley Jankowski   1C Ⓓ Sebastiany Branding & Design Ⓒ COPEL   1D Ⓓ Britt Funderburk Ⓒ Britt Funderburk

2A Ⓓ Sebastiany Branding & Design Ⓒ Keb   2B Ⓓ DTM_INC Ⓒ Paperstreet   2C Ⓓ AT PACE Ⓒ Lula Flat Pack Furniture   2D Ⓓ Chris Rooney Illustration/Design Ⓒ National Geographic Kids

3A Ⓓ Hazen Creative, Inc. Ⓒ Overcoat Management/Iron and Wine   3B Ⓓ Stefan Romanu Ⓒ self   3C Ⓓ Double O Design Ⓒ Kids Argentina   3D Ⓓ Cerny Product Development, Inc. Ⓒ Kinsco LLC

4A Ⓓ Chris Rooney Illustration/Design Ⓒ Vyyo   4B Ⓓ RetroMetro Designs Ⓒ Steve Moon   4C Ⓓ Just Creative Design Ⓒ LogoBlog   4D Ⓓ milou Ⓒ doop

5A Ⓓ dialog Ⓒ KokoPio   5B Ⓓ Kuznetsov Evgeniy | KUZNETS Ⓒ Rich-Kich.ru   5C Ⓓ Seven25 Design & Typography Ⓒ LOUD Foundation   5D Ⓓ tarsadia hotels Ⓒ mojo yogurt

LOGO SEARCH

Keywords **Calligraphy**

◯ Symbol   ◯ Typographic   ◯ Combo   ⦿ All

 1

 2

 3

 4

 5

Ⓟ = Design Firm   Ⓒ = Client

1C Ⓟ Gary Sample Design Ⓒ Jallick   1D Ⓟ Twhite Ⓒ Billabong

2A Ⓟ Rocket Science Ⓒ Stegmaier Brewing Company   2B Ⓟ Tran Creative Ⓒ Karma Coffee   2C Ⓟ The Brandit Ⓒ Deschutes Brewery   2D Ⓟ The Brandit Ⓒ One Twice

3A Ⓟ Nordyke Design Ⓒ Entwyned   3B Ⓟ Bauerhaus Design, Inc. Ⓒ Jenny & Steve Emerson   3C Ⓟ Insight Marketing Design Ⓒ Ambrosia Artistic Accents   3D Ⓟ Sabingrafik, Inc. Ⓒ Beverly Hills Hotel

4A Ⓟ MINE Ⓒ Christopher Simmons   4B Ⓟ Logoguppy Ⓒ John Mascarenhas   4C Ⓟ The Office of Art+Logik Ⓒ Inner Circle Enterprises   4D Ⓟ The Creative Method Ⓒ Over The Moon Dairy Co.

5A Ⓟ S Design Inc. Ⓒ Camp VanCamp Clothing Design   5B Ⓟ artproba creative solutions asia Ⓒ Roskonditer   5C Ⓟ Muhina Design Ⓒ Family Medicine   5D Ⓟ R&R Partners Ⓒ LVCVA

	A	B	C	D
1				
2				
3				
4				
5				

Ⓓ = Design Firm Ⓒ = Client

1A Ⓓ Schwartzrock Graphic Arts Ⓒ BI 1B Ⓓ Zieldesign Ⓒ Tremolat 1C Ⓓ Riley Designs Ⓒ Riley Hutchens 1D Ⓓ RICH design studio Ⓒ Radio City

2A Ⓓ Fezlab Ⓒ Eos Enterprises 2B Ⓓ Factor Tres Ⓒ Liverpool department store 2C Ⓓ Factor Tres Ⓒ Kimberly 2D Ⓓ David Clark Design Ⓒ Hard Rock Casino & Hotel

3A Ⓓ Mindgruve Ⓒ Visit Carlsbad 3B Ⓓ A.D. Creative Group Ⓒ Northern Hotel 3C Ⓓ united* Ⓒ united* 3D Ⓓ D*MN Good Ⓒ Mali

4A Ⓓ RocketDog Communications Ⓒ Fase 4B Ⓓ Label Brand Ⓒ Trident Design 4C Ⓓ mabu Ⓒ GoodGuy Brewery 4D Ⓓ LOWE-SSP3 S.A. Ⓒ Helm Bank

5A Ⓓ Schwartzrock Graphic Arts Ⓒ Design Center 5B Ⓓ Darling Design Ⓒ Courtney Darling 5C Ⓓ Ghiath Lahham Ⓒ PRIVATE 5D Ⓓ Boxon Vision Ⓒ Atyaf

Begucci
Identity Start-up

Paradox Box, Ufa, Russia

Designers at Paradox Box actually used coffee and tea to create a menagerie of animals for the new take-out coffee brand, Begucci.

Paradox Box was recently faced with a design assignment that many design firms around the world have tackled in the past decade: to create a new coffee shop brand. As the coffee/tea/chai trend continues to develop worldwide, the ability to stand out becomes more and more challenging. These drinks are considered by many to be a commodity item, so the personality of the brand itself becomes increasingly important.

The Begucci brand will be a take-out store located in Russian shopping centers. The positioning, concept, and naming were left entirely to the Paradox Box team.

"The brand name is a newly coined word based on the root of the Russian word *beg,* which means 'run.' The brand slogan that we created, *Dyla begutchikh po delam,* which means 'For those who are running on their business matters,' continues with the concept of running," explains Ilshat Baiburin, art director of Paradox Box.

The idea of running came through strongly in the new Begucci identity. Pictures of running animals, some fast and some slow, appear to be coming from spilled tea or coffee blobs. In truth, the animal art was actually created by painting with real blots of coffee and tea on white paper. Each was scanned and retouched to perfection.

About twenty different characters appeared from the blobs, including a kangaroo, reindeer, snail, tortoise, and bear, among others.

Next to each animal is a block of text written to further involve the cup holder with the brand. For example, next to the kangaroo image is this: "For those who are running on their business matters: to buy a new bag; to take a new height at one jump; to be on time for appointments; to make presents; to jump into the art gallery; to remember why we need to be there; to run further."

"The playful characters in the brand make it possible to involve the customer in a sort of game, and they contribute to the bright, unique, handmade style of the brand," the designer says.

LOGO SEARCH

Keywords: **Crests**

Type: ○ Symbol   ○ Typographic   ○ Combo   ● All

Ⓓ = Design Firm   Ⓒ = Client

1C Ⓓ Jon Kay Design Ⓒ Fangamer   1D Ⓓ gtc media Ⓒ Alfonso Duran

2A Ⓓ Sniff Design Studio Ⓒ Lucky Dog Coffee Company   2B Ⓓ Matchstic Ⓒ NTMA   2C Ⓓ Dotzero Design Ⓒ Dotzero   2D Ⓓ Majorminor Ⓒ Jeffrey and Kate Tanhueco

3A Ⓓ Voicebox Creative Ⓒ Trinchero Family Wines   3B Ⓓ Landor Associates Ⓒ Jane Goodall Good for all   3C Ⓓ Bryan Cooper Design Ⓒ Bryan Cooper   3D Ⓓ Sunday Lounge Ⓒ Colorado Boy Pub & Brewery

4A Ⓓ Tactix Creative Ⓒ Paul Howalt   4B Ⓓ Tim Frame Design Ⓒ Brothers Carpet Cleaning   4C Ⓓ 3 Advertising LLC Ⓒ 3 Advertising   4D Ⓓ Level B Design Ⓒ Café Max

5A Ⓓ Sussner Design Company Ⓒ Sussner Design Co   5B Ⓓ Gardner Design Ⓒ self   5C Ⓓ PUSH Branding and Design Ⓒ Wellmark BCBS & Drake Relays   5D Ⓓ Design Hub Ⓒ Lb. Brewing Co.

	A	B	C	D
1				
2				
3				
4				
5				

Ⓓ = Design Firm   Ⓒ = Client

1A Ⓓ Sandra Murray Design Ⓒ Tamales Mexican Grill 1B Ⓓ Caliente Creative Ⓒ Bay Harbor Fine Foods 1C Ⓓ PUSH Branding and Design Ⓒ Iowa State Fair 1D Ⓓ PUSH Branding and Design Ⓒ Boxwoods

2A Ⓓ fugasi creative Ⓒ Austintatious Blinds and Shutters 2B Ⓓ BRUEDESIGN Ⓒ Capture Studios 2C Ⓓ jonskaggs.com Ⓒ Healthy Express 2D Ⓓ 3 Advertising LLC Ⓒ The National Museum of Nuclear Science & History

3A Ⓓ Brian Haselton Ⓒ The Whirling Whisk Baking Co. 3B Ⓓ Chris Herron Design Ⓒ NHH Confections 3C Ⓓ The Robin Shepherd Group Ⓒ Sweet N Flour 3D Ⓓ Sudduth Design Co. Ⓒ Deep Eddy Distilling Co.

4A Ⓓ Heisel Design Ⓒ The Calm Coming 4B Ⓓ Stiles Design Ⓒ Annies Cafe & Bar 4C Ⓓ Glitschka Studios Ⓒ DeHann Holsteins 4D Ⓓ Gardner Design Ⓒ Cufflinks.com

5A Ⓓ Gerren Lamson Ⓒ Stonebridge Outdoor 5B Ⓓ Stiles Design Ⓒ The Butler Bros./LAF 5C Ⓓ Limelight Advertising & Design Ⓒ Brimacombe 5D Ⓓ POLLARDdesign Ⓒ Greenhouse

	A	B	C	D
1				
2				
3				
4				
5				

ⅅ = Design Firm   ⅽ = Client

1A ⅅ Marketsplash by HP ⅽ Boise Fire Department   1B ⅅ Stiles Design ⅽ Wurstfest   1C ⅅ Flying Hand Media ⅽ NC Lit Festival   1D ⅅ Design Hub ⅽ Lb. Brewing Co.

2A ⅅ Combustion ⅽ FatTone   2B ⅅ 3 Advertising LLC ⅽ AloneAndUnafraid.com   2C ⅅ a. pounds design ⅽ Oak Cliff Bicycle Company   2D ⅅ moosylvania ⅽ Bacardi

3A ⅅ Schwartzrock Graphic Arts ⅽ Blackwood Management Group   3B ⅅ Timber Design Company ⅽ LaCrosse Footwear   3C ⅅ Spring Advertising + Design ⅽ Joey Restaurant Group   3D ⅅ Mattson Creative ⅽ CS Lewis College

4A ⅅ markatos | moore ⅽ Ambassador   4B ⅅ FUEL Creative Group ⅽ The Sacramento Press   4C ⅅ Blacktop Creative ⅽ Blacktop Creative   4D ⅅ Jon Kay Design ⅽ Fangamer

5A ⅅ Jon Kay Design ⅽ Fangamer   5B ⅅ Gardner Design ⅽ Horace Mann Dual Language Magnet School   5C ⅅ Cubic ⅽ BOK Center   5D ⅅ Glitschka Studios ⅽ Mardi Gras World

A	B	C	D	
				1
				2
				3
				4
				5

Ⓓ = Design Firm   Ⓒ = Client

1A Ⓓ Letter+Five Ⓒ Brushed Monkey   1B Ⓓ phyx design Ⓒ phish   1C Ⓓ Barral Ⓒ Harmonie intérieure   1D Ⓓ Sol Consultores Ⓒ Tutti Gelatti

2A Ⓓ 903 Creative, LLC Ⓒ Gibson - Lewis Family   2B Ⓓ Karl Design Vienna Ⓒ SC Berarium srl Romania   2C Ⓓ Tomko Design Ⓒ SFT Tequila Bar   2D Ⓓ Deutsch Design Works Ⓒ Anheuser Busch InBev

3A Ⓓ TOKY Branding+Design Ⓒ Photobooth Planet   3B Ⓓ Unreal Ⓒ Cortland Partners   3C Ⓓ Toolbox Creative Ⓒ Tom Campbell   3D Ⓓ 484 Design, Inc. Ⓒ Leon Etienne Magic Products

4A Ⓓ Ullman Design Ⓒ E&D's Cukoo Uhrens   4B Ⓓ Bauerhaus Design, Inc. Ⓒ Canine Country   4C Ⓓ Chen Design Associates Ⓒ Verve Coffee Roasters   4D Ⓓ fugasi creative Ⓒ CAKE high-end events

5A Ⓓ Scott Oeschger Ⓒ M&M   5B Ⓓ Ptarmak, Inc. Ⓒ Honest Don's   5C Ⓓ Oxide Design Co. Ⓒ Pitch coal-fire pizzeria   5D Ⓓ Scott Oeschger Ⓒ M&M

Eat Innovations
Identity Design

Ptarmak, Austin, Texas

If you invented a new food product and wanted to bring it to market, Eat Innovations would be the sort of company you'd like to partner with. With offices in Newport Beach, California, and New York City, the young company offers a full menu of competencies—advice on flavor profiles, knowledge about the competition, sales and brokerage abilities, package design resources, delivery capabilities, brand maintenance, and more.

"For the small guy or young entrepreneur, that kind of advice can be priceless," explains J. R. Crosby, founder of Ptarmak (pronounced "tarmac"). "Eat can take your ideas out of the conceptual realm and put it in the hands of real-world consumers."

For the client's identity, having to reference all of those competencies—including the fact that Eat Innovations specializes in natural products—was a challenge. But it was a very important challenge to meet. There is plenty of competition in the consumer product development category, so a vague logo wouldn't stand out enough or suggest how the client was unique. If the new design was overly specific—for example, if it focused too much on "natural"—it could pigeonhole the company.

"We needed the new logo to accomplish several things: communicate food, imply service, indicate ideation, convey progress along

the path toward achieving results, have it feel natural, and tap a fun/endearing personality," says Crosby. Of course, the client's memorable name also needed to play an important part.

The Ptarmak team explored a wide range of ideas, including plenty of applicable clichés—food for thought, brainstorming, give me something to chew on, and so on—searching for concepts that could go visual but also to find that right balance between cliché (boring) and the familiar (understandable).

The Eat logo, by Ptarmak, is a sly mix of wordmark and graphics, with several layers of meaning.

Their final solution brought many familiar visual concepts together in a new and unexpected way. Forming the negative space in the e of "eat" is a combination bite mark/thought bubble/(brain)storm cloud, aptly placed above a serving spoon that forms a path—an indication of progress—into the negative space of the a. The sexy path down the back of the a points right at the other key word, "Innovations," which is appropriately set in a neutral typeface.

The color scheme indicates "natural," and its gradation gives a sense of progression. The letterspacing, quirkily spaced for optical appropriateness rather than mathematical spacing, makes the wordmark endearing and memorable.

LOGO SEARCH

Keywords **Sports**

Type: ◯ Symbol   ◯ Typographic   ◯ Combo   ● All

REMEMBER

ⓓ = Design Firm   ⓒ = Client

1C ⓓ RARE Design ⓒ Richfield Renegades Baseball Club 1D ⓓ RARE Design ⓒ Xtreme Baseball Club

2A ⓓ RARE Design ⓒ Xtreme Baseball Club 2B ⓓ Chameleon Design Group, LLC ⓒ Doug Carroll Baseball Academy 2C ⓓ iHook Creative ⓒ Matt Faulk 2D ⓓ Fargo Design Co., Inc. ⓒ Fred McGriff

3A ⓓ Skye Design Studios ⓒ Springfield Sliders 3B ⓓ Strange Ideas ⓒ James Strange 3C ⓓ Sunday Lounge ⓒ Salida High School 3D ⓓ Torch Creative ⓒ NBA Entertainment

4A ⓓ LindyLazar Marketing ⓒ Jamo Memorial 4B ⓓ Campbell Fisher Design ⓒ BDA Sports 4C ⓓ Aurum Design ⓒ WNBA 4D ⓓ Campbell Fisher Design ⓒ BDA Sports

5A ⓓ RARE Design ⓒ personal 5B ⓓ RARE Design ⓒ Personal 5C ⓓ Little Box Of Ideas ⓒ Jay Patel 5D ⓓ Tactix Creative ⓒ NFL Planet

	A	B	C	D
1				
2				
3				
4				
5				—

Ⓓ = Design Firm   Ⓒ = Client

1A Ⓓ Gyula Nemeth Ⓒ Saskatchewan Roughriders   1B Ⓓ Jason Drumheller Ⓒ Towson University   1C Ⓓ Gyula Nemeth Ⓒ Pro Football Magazine   1D Ⓓ Combustion Ⓒ Muhammad Ali Enterprises

2A Ⓓ Patten ID Ⓒ CASL   2B Ⓓ KENNETH DISEÑO Ⓒ Maripepas Soccer Team   2C Ⓓ DikranianDesign Ⓒ Florida Youth Soccer Association   2D Ⓓ Double A Creative Ⓒ TNJG

3A Ⓓ AHEAD Ⓒ GOLF FIGHTS CANCER   3B Ⓓ Marketsplash by HP Ⓒ Logoworks   3C Ⓓ Tran Creative Ⓒ Coeur d'Alene Golf Shop   3D Ⓓ Gobranding.eu Ⓒ Face to Face

4A Ⓓ Banowetz + Company, Inc. Ⓒ Benji Homsey   4B Ⓓ Jeff Kern Design Ⓒ Bogey's Golf Apparel   4C Ⓓ Pierpoint Design + Branding Ⓒ Tennis Without Borders   4D Ⓓ Unreal Ⓒ American Heart Association

5A Ⓓ Asgard Ⓒ Bowling City   5B Ⓓ Sudduth Design Co. Ⓒ Continental Mills   5C Ⓓ Gyula Nemeth Ⓒ Ironhead   5D Ⓓ Iconologic Ⓒ Torino Organizing Committee

LOGO SEARCH

Keywords **Heads**

Type: ◯ Symbol ◯ Typographic ◯ Combo ⦿ All

SEEDS OF STRENGTH

Ⓓ = Design Firm   Ⓒ = Client

1C Ⓓ Ryan Russell Design Ⓒ Snooty Peacock   1D Ⓓ Graphismo Ⓒ Seeds of Strength

2A Ⓓ BrandBerry Ⓒ TravelWorld.su   2B Ⓓ Device Ⓒ Mercury Records   2C Ⓓ Device Ⓒ Device   2D Ⓓ Graphismo Ⓒ Wonderful Things

3A Ⓓ Device Ⓒ Rian Hughes   3B Ⓓ The Robin Shepherd Group Ⓒ TigerLily Media   3C Ⓓ Device Ⓒ Device   3D Ⓓ PUSH Branding and Design Ⓒ Big Head Joe

4A Ⓓ Porkka & Kuutsa Oy Ⓒ Corbel Oy   4B Ⓓ 01d Ⓒ Anti Glamour Legion   4C Ⓓ Combustion Ⓒ Muhammad Ali Enterprises   4D Ⓓ Gyula Nemeth Ⓒ Ironhead

5A Ⓓ X3 Studios Ⓒ Teta   5B Ⓓ Sakideamsheni Ⓒ George Bokhua   5C Ⓓ Sakideamsheni Ⓒ Esthetic Education   5D Ⓓ M. Brady Clark Design Ⓒ salsasavant.com

	A	B	C	D
1				
2			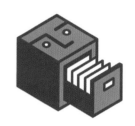	
3				
4				
5				

D = Design Firm   C = Client

1A D Sol Consultores C Fundacion Vigas   1B D Christopher Dina C Museum (Proposed)   1C D Hive Communication C Nathan Betts   1D D The Joe Bosack Graphic Design Co. C Xavier University

2A D Gobranding.eu C Wojciech Janicki   2B D Gyula Nemeth C Amusement Park Budapest   2C D 01d C Picabinet   2D D Design Army C Virginia Film Festival

3A D BBDO Branding C Moscow International Advertising Festival Red Apple   3B D Brent Couchman Design C ACU   3C D 01d C Gohead!   3D D Gardner Design C Quiz Bowl Brainiacs

4A D Combustion C Muhammad Ali Enterprises   4B D Wizemark C PlanetGum   4C D A.D. Creative Group C Billings OB-GYN Associates   4D D Nectar Graphics C Mes Amies

5A D Evenson Design Group C Sound Mind Music   5B D Jarek Kowalczyk C personal   5C D Strange Ideas C James Strange   5D D POLLARDdesign C PleaseMerge.com

	A	B	C	D	
1					1
2					2
3	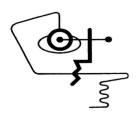				3
4					4
5					5

Ⓓ = Design Firm   Ⓒ = Client

1A Ⓓ Duffy & Partners Ⓒ Wolfgang Puck   1B Ⓓ Nynas Ⓒ three eyed bros   1C Ⓓ lunabrand design group Ⓒ Market Street Toffee   1D Ⓓ LeBoYe Ⓒ dialogue cafe

2A Ⓓ 01d Ⓒ GlowingMind.net   2B Ⓓ 903 Creative, LLC Ⓒ Homeland Security Outlook   2C Ⓓ Suprematika Ⓒ Doctor head   2D Ⓓ Ferreira Design Company Ⓒ Ferreira Design Company

3A Ⓓ Schwartzrock Graphic Arts Ⓒ Design Center   3B Ⓓ Sommese Design Ⓒ The Penn State Singers   3C Ⓓ Essex Two Ⓒ MASQUE Boutique   3D Ⓓ El Paso, Galeria de Comunicacion Ⓒ Silvia PÃ(c)rez

4A Ⓓ Strange Ideas Ⓒ James Strange   4B Ⓓ Strange Ideas Ⓒ James Strange   4C Ⓓ Strange Ideas Ⓒ James Strange   4D Ⓓ SUPERRED Ⓒ Andreas

5A Ⓓ Studio Ink Ⓒ RoomNinja   5B Ⓓ Sean Heisler Ⓒ Smartzio   5C Ⓓ Refinery Design Company Ⓒ Tri-State Drug Task Force   5D Ⓓ IDEGRAFO Ⓒ Origyn Fertility Center

	A	B	C	D
1				
2				
3				
4				
5				

Ⓓ = Design Firm   Ⓒ = Client

1A Ⓓ Make Area Ⓒ Detector   1B Ⓓ BRUEDESIGN Ⓒ BRUEDESIGN   1C Ⓓ Z&G Ⓒ Alexandr Kalganov   1D Ⓓ Mattson Creative Ⓒ Discovery Channel

2A Ⓓ mIQelangelo Ⓒ Invision   2B Ⓓ Klik-Dizajn Ⓒ Klik-Dizajn graphic design   2C Ⓓ Deep See Design Ⓒ Knot Heads Hair Accesories With a Twist   2D Ⓓ RED The Agency Ⓒ LuluBelle Gluten-free Gourmet

3A Ⓓ 01d Ⓒ LDportal   3B Ⓓ Tom Robinson Graphic Design Ⓒ Circle Ten Events   3C Ⓓ Bailey Lauerman Ⓒ James Strange   3D Ⓓ Univisual Ⓒ Mixura

4A Ⓓ The Brand Hatchery Ⓒ WideEye Interactive   4B Ⓓ Identity33 Ⓒ Frey Vision Group   4C Ⓓ Felixsockwell.com Ⓒ time   4D Ⓓ PLAY Creative Ⓒ PLAY Creative

5A Ⓓ Molly McCoy Ⓒ Berkeley Student Food Collective   5B Ⓓ Kevin Zwirble Design Co. Ⓒ Legendary Masterminds   5C Ⓓ 3 Advertising LLC Ⓒ Mercy Regional Hospital   5D Ⓓ Propaganda Inc. Ⓒ Nawgan

Alhurra
Identity Design

C&G Partners, New York, New York

"Freedom of information" might not be a phrase many people would associate with Arabic media. But that concept is at the core of an identity C&G Partners created for Alhurra (Arabic for "The Free One"), a commercial-free Arabic language satellite television network in the Middle East devoted to news and information. It is a network financed by the United States, intended to respectfully provide a young pan-Arabic audience with unbiased news and information without appearing to be overly Arabic.

"It was a special challenge to work in a completely foreign language, including letterforms and typography. It was very important to understand and comprehend a different sensibility and culture where water and fluidity is very important," explains Steff Geissbuhler of C&G Partners.

A multicolored bird in flight, built from three flowing ribbons, clearly communicated freedom, creativity, and multinationalism. The bird flies upward, toward freedom and light. The yellow, red, and purple ribbons speak of celebration, like flags or banners. Geissbuhler decided to keep the supporting typography from the network's original identity, which provided a connection for loyal viewers to the new identity.

The bird is dynamic as a static logo, but it comes alive in animation. The three ribbons separate from each other, swirling and flying, each on its own forward-moving course. They interact with typography, photos, and film footage, sometimes reassembling into the bird logo and sometimes emphasizing visuals such as frames or underlines. They can also be combined as graphical elements into complex patterning.

The three ribbons in Alhurra's new logo, created by C&G Partners, are easily animated, patterned, and otherwise rearranged in many identity applications.

Arab viewers know that this is a U.S. network, just like CNN and CNBC, or the English BBC. "All are broadcasting in that space as well and have Arabic language programming. The main aim was to look different from Al Jazeera, Al Arabia, Abu Dhabi, and others—more colorful, animated, and young—and yes, somewhat American," Geissbuhler notes.

For network news, the bird is shown in red only, which conveys a greater sense of seriousness and urgency. For the network's *Today* show applications, the bird is delineated with just two lines or ribbons on a field of gold, The idea was to give this program a separate but related identity and color scheme.

Creative director: Steff Geissbuhler, partner, C&G Partners
Animators and production company: The String Theory

	A	B	C	D

1

LOGO SEARCH

Keywords **People**

Type: ○ Symbol ○ Typographic ○ Combo ● All

U.S. VIRGIN ISLANDS™
st.CROIX st.JOHN st.THOMAS

BLACK ROCK

2

ASGARD

Fleuret
DE ST.PETERSBOURG

african hunter
EXCLUSIVE HUNTING SAFARIS

3

DEL PESTO
PIZZA DELIVERY SERVICE

DEL PESTO
ДОСТАВКА ПИЦЦЫ

Control Your Cash

ALBANATOR

4

orange

↗ Fitlist.ru

5

Billings
OB GYN
ASSOCIATES

клиника ♥
Здоров Я!

OBGYN
of London

Ⓓ = Design Firm Ⓒ = Client

1C Ⓓ Iconologic Ⓒ US Virgin Islands 1D Ⓓ Schwartzrock Graphic Arts Ⓒ BlackRock Graphics

2A Ⓓ Schwartzrock Graphic Arts Ⓒ Delphax Technologies 2B Ⓓ Asgard Ⓒ Asgard 2C Ⓓ Asgard Ⓒ St. Petersburg Open 2D Ⓓ KarbonBlack Creative Ⓒ African Hunter

3A Ⓓ 01d Ⓒ Sushcof 3B Ⓓ 01d Ⓒ Suchcof 3C Ⓓ R&R Partners Ⓒ Greg McFarlane 3D Ⓓ KW43 BRANDDESIGN Ⓒ RTI Sports GmbH

4A Ⓓ 01d Ⓒ 2Orange.ru 4B Ⓓ Schwartzrock Graphic Arts Ⓒ Wiese Creative 4C Ⓓ Spring Interactive Ⓒ Digitalmind Ltd. 4D Ⓓ seekvisum graphics Ⓒ fitlist.ru

5A Ⓓ A.D. Creative Group Ⓒ Billings OB-GYN Associates 5B Ⓓ Muhina Design Ⓒ clinic Zdorov'ya 5C Ⓓ LogoDesignGuru.com Ⓒ M.Waqas Iqbal 5D Ⓓ cultiva Ⓒ Obstetrics and Gynecology of London

A	B	C	D	
				1

				2
				3
				4
				5

Ⓓ = Design Firm   Ⓒ = Client

1A Ⓓ Glitschka Studios Ⓒ nPulse Networks   1B Ⓓ Paradox Box Ⓒ DJ Alex   1C Ⓓ Glitschka Studios Ⓒ Joystick Warriors   1D Ⓓ Device Ⓒ Device

2A Ⓓ Oxide Design Co. Ⓒ Society for Geek Advancement   2B Ⓓ Glitschka Studios Ⓒ Street Level Adventures   2C Ⓓ Whaley Design, Ltd Ⓒ Feist Animal Hospital   2D Ⓓ Glitschka Studios Ⓒ KZ Creative

3A Ⓓ Schwartzrock Graphic Arts Ⓒ Eason and Associates   3B Ⓓ Yatta Yatta Yatta Ⓒ Impact Zone Photography   3C Ⓓ Flight Deck Creative Ⓒ Mark Voss   3D Ⓓ DUSTIN PARKER ARTS Ⓒ Young Chefs

4A Ⓓ Freshwater Design Ⓒ Babz Wilkins   4B Ⓓ Whaley Design, Ltd Ⓒ Feist Animal Hospital   4C Ⓓ XY ARTS Ⓒ Quan   4D Ⓓ Schwartzrock Graphic Arts Ⓒ Wiese Creative

5A Ⓓ Kommunikat Ⓒ Jakub Rutkowski   5B Ⓓ Kuznetsov Evgeniy | KUZNETS Ⓒ Dance academy   5C Ⓓ Noesis Ⓒ Ol Malo Trust   5D Ⓓ Hibblen Design Ⓒ Salvador's Deli

	A	B	C	D
1				
2				
3				
4				
5				

ⓓ = Design Firm   ⓒ = Client

1A ⓓ Schwartzrock Graphic Arts ⓒ Design Center   1B ⓓ Glitschka Studios ⓒ InContext   1C ⓓ R&R Partners ⓒ Randy Heil   1D ⓓ Luxecetera, Inc. ⓒ Ann Westerman Photography

2A ⓓ Oleg Peters ⓒ Okko   2B ⓓ Diana Graham ⓒ ERnst + ANgelika inDIA   2C ⓓ Hotbed Creative ⓒ Breathe In Yoga   2D ⓓ Cassie Klingler Design ⓒ Music Birth Therapy

3A ⓓ RawType ⓒ Jacob's Well   3B ⓓ Strange Ideas ⓒ James Strange   3C ⓓ JRDG Brand Design & Communications ⓒ Amnesty International / Chiat Day   3D ⓓ Strange Ideas ⓒ James Strange

4A ⓓ M3 Advertising Design ⓒ ThreeSquare.org   4B ⓓ Sean Heisler ⓒ Sean Heisler   4C ⓓ brandclay ⓒ Cloud 9   4D ⓓ RedSpark Creative Ltd ⓒ People Publishing Ltd

5A ⓓ Roy Smith Design ⓒ World Moto   5B ⓓ Double A Creative ⓒ Swanson Russell   5C ⓓ Deney ⓒ Municipality of Kadikoy   5D ⓓ Vanessa AdÃo ⓒ Lanteq

A	B	C	D	
				1
				2
				3
				4
				5

Ⓓ = Design Firm   Ⓒ = Client

1A Ⓓ Logorado Ⓒ Knockout   1B Ⓓ McMillian Design Ⓒ Shop Keep   1C Ⓓ EXPLORARE Ⓒ Introspecta Consultores   1D Ⓓ Joan Pons Moll Ⓒ Jangha

2A Ⓓ Citizen Studio Ⓒ Sega Song   2B Ⓓ concussion, llc Ⓒ Yuru   2C Ⓓ LOCHS Ⓒ University of Amsterdam   2D Ⓓ alekchmura.com Ⓒ 4 Fitness Boxing

3A Ⓓ GripNStay LLC Ⓒ Sandon Spalding   3B Ⓓ R&R Partners Ⓒ R&R Partners   3C Ⓓ Hayes Image Ⓒ Illy Baby   3D Ⓓ Gizwiz Studio Ⓒ Black Ninja Software

4A Ⓓ d-signbureau Ⓒ Matthias Schilling   4B Ⓓ 01d Ⓒ Sushcof   4C Ⓓ Anna Kovecses Ⓒ kor hatarok nelkul   4D Ⓓ Little Box Of Ideas Ⓒ Imported Mexican Foods

5A Ⓓ Joan Pons Moll Ⓒ uReach Media   5B Ⓓ Niedermeier Design Ⓒ Yo Lassi   5C Ⓓ Sanders Design Ⓒ McDonald Tinker   5D Ⓓ RedBrand Ⓒ Evgeniy Golovach

	A	**B**	**C**	**D**
1				
2				
3				
4				
5				

D = Design Firm **C** = Client

1A **D** The Creative System **C** Athena Construction Group 1B **D** 01d **C** Status 1C **D** 3 Advertising LLC **C** New Mexico Advertising Federation 1D **D** Judson Design **C** spec

2A **D** TOKY Branding+Design **C** St. Louis Jazz Festival 2B **D** Balcom Agency **C** Santa Fe Youth Services 2C **D** Sakideamsheni **C** George Bokhua 2D **D** Ryan Kegley **C** Tulsa Ballet

3A **D** Dotzero Design **C** Poco Pictures 3B **D** Igor Duibanov **C** Armored Stripes 3C **D** Rispler&Rispler Designer Partnerschaftsgesellschaf **C** Redplane Business Coaching 3D **D** Gearbox **C** Lonely Grange Recorders

4A **D** Dara Creative **C** CFM Group 4B **D** Anthony Lane Studios **C** Ryan Johnson 4C **D** Niedermeier Design **C** Windy City Wine Guy 4D **D** Niedermeier Design **C** Windy City Wine Guy

5A **D** Gavula Design Associates **C** Stamford Hospital 5B **D** Gröters Design **C** Caritas GAP 5C **D** Stitch Design Co. **C** Eve Simone 5D **D** More Branding+Communication **C** Child Abuse Network (CAN)

	A	B	C	D	
1			grips		1
2					2
3					3
4					4
5					5

 = Design Firm Ⓒ = Client

1A Ⓓ Canyon Creative Ⓒ Nannies & Housekeepers U.S.A.   1B Ⓓ identity kitchen Ⓒ identity kitchen   1C Ⓓ XY ARTS Ⓒ Grips International   1D Ⓓ Rachel Castor Ⓒ Fashion for Music

2A Ⓓ Niedermeier Design Ⓒ Blacksmith Brands   2B Ⓓ Logo Design Works Ⓒ Slice Fixer   2C Ⓓ Caliber Creative, LLC Ⓒ Caliber Creative   2D Ⓓ Design Army Ⓒ Rockport

3A Ⓓ Design Army Ⓒ Rockport   3B Ⓓ SGNL Studio Ⓒ DUEL Purpose   3C Ⓓ Gardner Design Ⓒ WSU Alumni Association   3D Ⓓ Deep See Design Ⓒ Peter Jones

4A Ⓓ KONZEPT DESIGN ILLU Ⓒ punktgenau GmbH/ Westfalenhallen Dortmund GmbH   4B Ⓓ Heisel Design Ⓒ Sarasota City Park Foundation   4C Ⓓ Thinking*Room Inc. Ⓒ Plaza Indonesia

4D Ⓓ Swingset-Imagination Ⓒ Swingset Imagination   5A Ⓓ Device Ⓒ Rian Hughes   5B Ⓓ David Gramblin Ⓒ David Gramblin   5C Ⓓ Kuznetsov Evgeniy | KUZNETS Ⓒ Dance Academy

5D Ⓓ Matthew Wells Design Ⓒ Vancouver Ultimate League

	A	**B**	**C**	**D**
1		 Good Will Running	 401k Latte	
2		 connectME		
3				
4				
5				

Ⓓ = Design Firm   Ⓒ = Client

1A Ⓓ 01d Ⓒ Ministry of Joy 1B Ⓓ Allison Emery Creative Ⓒ Allison Emery 1C Ⓓ Schwartzrock Graphic Arts Ⓒ 401k Latte 1D Ⓓ Schwartzrock Graphic Arts Ⓒ AIGA Minnesota

2A Ⓓ LogoDesignGuru.com Ⓒ Tajdar Sultan 2B Ⓓ ARGUS Ⓒ Connect Me 2C Ⓓ Dickerson Ⓒ Marcus Dickerson 2D Ⓓ R&R Partners Ⓒ Randy Heil

3A Ⓓ Felixsockwell.com Ⓒ prospect presbyterian 3B Ⓓ Mission Minded Ⓒ Hope SF 3C Ⓓ Kessler Design Group Ⓒ Sister to Sister Foundation 3D Ⓓ Glitschka Studios Ⓒ Thread Connect

4A Ⓓ Rizoma Identidad Visual Ⓒ Swisscontact 4B Ⓓ Sakideamsheni Ⓒ george bokhua 4C Ⓓ Sunday Lounge Ⓒ Ubiquity Group / Gambro 4D Ⓓ Andrea Nassar Ⓒ Hasbaya Festival

5A Ⓓ Eiland Design Ⓒ Community Roundtable 5B Ⓓ Rizoma Identidad Visual Ⓒ CARE Ecuador 5C Ⓓ Niedermeier Design Ⓒ Village Pediatric Cardiology 5D Ⓓ J Fletcher Design Ⓒ IOA Connect

	A	B	C	D
1	 Chocolate Man			
2	 ecovise		 naturehand	 urbanroots
3	HelpHaiti	halt		
4	socius 		CityCliq	
5	 idApostle			 Handmade КАФЕ

Ⓓ = Design Firm   Ⓒ = Client

1A Ⓓ DL Designs Ⓒ David Lambo   1B Ⓓ Voicebox Creative Ⓒ Teach with Africa   1C Ⓓ Alik Yakubovich agency Ⓒ Give Me Five!   1D Ⓓ Niedermeier Design Ⓒ Advanced Human Technologies

2A Ⓓ Anna Kovecses Ⓒ ecovise   2B Ⓓ Brent Couchman Design Ⓒ ACU   2C Ⓓ Dalius Stuoka Ⓒ Naturehand   2D Ⓓ dee duncan Ⓒ dee duncan

3A Ⓓ Wizemark Ⓒ 365 Logo Project   3B Ⓓ Roy Smith Design Ⓒ World Moto   3C Ⓓ Siah Design Ⓒ ASLplace.com   3D Ⓓ Felixsockwell.com Ⓒ arturo's

4A Ⓓ designproject Ⓒ Socius One Consulting   4B Ⓓ Siah Design Ⓒ Siah Design   4C Ⓓ rajasandhu.com Ⓒ CityCliq.com   4D Ⓓ Hole in the Roof Ⓒ Hey! Unite

5A Ⓓ idApostle Ⓒ idApostle   5B Ⓓ Schwartzrock Graphic Arts Ⓒ Werner Design Werks   5C Ⓓ Schwartzrock Graphic Arts Ⓒ Design Center   5D Ⓓ Sergey Shapiro Ⓒ Handmade Café

A	B	C	D

1

2

3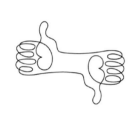

4

5

ⓓ = Design Firm   ⓒ = Client

1A ⓓ Gardner Design ⓒ Phoenix Productions   1B ⓓ Jase Neapolitan Design ⓒ American Landscape Preservation Group   1C ⓓ BrandExtract ⓒ Portfolio Resident Services   1D ⓓ Whaley Design, Ltd ⓒ Kevin Whaley

2A ⓓ Chad Mjos ⓒ Information Shared Networks   2B ⓓ Kommunikat ⓒ Daylight   2C ⓓ T&E Polydorou Design Ltd ⓒ Jenny Polydorou   2D ⓓ LeBoYe ⓒ Kartika Soekarno Foundation

3A ⓓ Felixsockwell.com ⓒ New York Times   3B ⓓ Ryan Kegley ⓒ L'union Fait La Force (Union Makes Strength)   3C ⓓ Green Ink Studio ⓒ Randall Museum   3D ⓓ wray ward ⓒ give 4 charity

4A ⓓ Siah Design ⓒ Action Now International   4B ⓓ Schifino Lee Advertising ⓒ Nicolas Gomez   4C ⓓ Schwartzrock Graphic Arts ⓒ TorqueTec   4D ⓓ Chad Mjos ⓒ Hercules Tire Company

5A ⓓ Gibson ⓒ Sendster   5B ⓓ Oxide Design Co. ⓒ Word Made Flesh   5C ⓓ Juggler Design ⓒ OmniCrete - SureStone   5D ⓓ agregidea ⓒ Personal Project

LOGO SEARCH

Keywords   **Mythology**

○ Symbol ○ Typographic ○ Combo ● All

ⓓ = Design Firm ⓒ = Client

1C ⓓ Device ⓒ Device 1D ⓓ 01d ⓒ digbox.ru

2A ⓓ henriquez lara ⓒ Santos Diablitos 2B ⓓ Design Hub ⓒ Lb. Brewing Co. 2C ⓓ Storm Design Inc. ⓒ Factory 1969 2D ⓓ Jason Drumheller ⓒ Wings of the Commonwealth Motorcycle Club

3A ⓓ Chad Mjos ⓒ Littlefield 3B ⓓ Rick Landon Design ⓒ AnalogX 3C ⓓ Judson Design ⓒ Amnesty International 3D ⓓ Gyula Nemeth ⓒ Gyula Németh

4A ⓓ julian peck ⓒ julian peck 4B ⓓ a. pounds design ⓒ Tranquilo 4C ⓓ wray ward ⓒ self 4D ⓓ laurendesigns ⓒ laurendesigns promo

5A ⓓ Gyula Nemeth ⓒ Ironhead 5B ⓓ Grindell Design ⓒ Psyclemaniac Gear 5C ⓓ Clay McIntosh Creative ⓒ O.D. Davenport 5D ⓓ Device ⓒ Device

	A	**B**	**C**	**D**
1				
2				
3				
4				
5				

Ⓓ = Design Firm Ⓒ = Client

1A Ⓓ Sunday Lounge Ⓒ Monarch Mountain 1B Ⓓ alekchmura.com Ⓒ Alek Chmura 1C Ⓓ Dotzero Design Ⓒ Falcon Art Community 1D Ⓓ Dragon Lunchbox Ⓒ Matthew Holloway

2A Ⓓ Device Ⓒ Rian Hughes 2B Ⓓ insight design Ⓒ Hunt Realty 2C Ⓓ Device Ⓒ Device 2D Ⓓ Device Ⓒ Rian Hughes

3A Ⓓ RARE Design Ⓒ Personal 3B Ⓓ Glitschka Studios Ⓒ Muscle Ink 3C Ⓓ Gyula Nemeth Ⓒ Landshut Cannibals 3D Ⓓ Glitschka Studios Ⓒ Upper Deck Company

4A Ⓓ Theory Associates Ⓒ Franken Phile 4B Ⓓ Gyula Nemeth Ⓒ Walhalla Warriors 4C Ⓓ Rickabaugh Graphics Ⓒ Cornerstone Christian Schools 4D Ⓓ RARE Design Ⓒ Personal

5A Ⓓ Pixelube Ⓒ Intocica! 5B Ⓓ Glitschka Studios Ⓒ Veer 5C Ⓓ Dessein Ⓒ Red Tiki 5D Ⓓ Scott Oeschger Ⓒ Lucha Creative

A	B	C	D	
				1
				2
				3
				4
				5

Ⓓ = Design Firm   Ⓒ = Client

1A Ⓓ Device Ⓒ Device   1B Ⓓ Karl Design Vienna Ⓒ SC Berarium srl Romania   1C Ⓓ Cubic Ⓒ BOK Center   1D Ⓓ Home Grown Logos Ⓒ TheGraphicsFairy.com

2A Ⓓ Glitschka Studios Ⓒ Data Marketing Ltd.   2B Ⓓ Angel's Life   2C Ⓓ Strange Ideas Ⓒ James Strange   2D Ⓓ Mission Creative Ⓒ Half Door Records

3A Ⓓ Siren   3B Ⓓ RedBrand Ⓒ AltoMare   3C Ⓓ huebner petersen Ⓒ Indochine   3D Ⓓ a. pounds design Ⓒ Tranquilo

4A Ⓓ Shelby Designs & Illustrates Ⓒ Schuyler McGraw   4B Ⓓ Gardner Design Ⓒ Graphic Impressions   4C Ⓓ Imagine Creative Ⓒ Pegasus Communications   4D Ⓓ Troyca - Visual Solutions GmbH Ⓒ Geiger Raumkonzepte

5A Ⓓ Orange Label Ⓒ Promtechgaz   5B Ⓓ crookedjaw design Ⓒ crookedjaw design   5C Ⓓ Alphabet Arm Design Ⓒ Elly Hartshorn & Josh McFadden   5D Ⓓ catherine blomkamp Ⓒ Hammersmith & Elephant

1

2

3

4

5

Ⓓ = Design Firm Ⓒ = Client

1A Ⓓ Device Ⓒ Device 1B Ⓓ Device Ⓒ Device 1C Ⓓ Design Army Ⓒ VA Film Festival 1D Ⓓ Device Ⓒ Device

2A Ⓓ X3 Studios Ⓒ Lista lu 2B Ⓓ Logoholik Ⓒ Bojan Stefanovic 2C Ⓓ POLLARDdesign Ⓒ Zookeeper 2D Ⓓ Glitschka Studios Ⓒ BAM Agency

3A Ⓓ Orange Label Ⓒ Fidelity Advertisment 3B Ⓓ Device Ⓒ DC Comics 3C Ⓓ Nadim Twal Ⓒ Maen Abu Taleb 3D Ⓓ Taylor Vanden Hoek Ⓒ Muskegon Lumberjacks

4A Ⓓ XY ARTS Ⓒ Sesseo 4B Ⓓ Gyula Nemeth Ⓒ Robot Webdesigner 4C Ⓓ NewCity Ⓒ ToyBright 4D Ⓓ Strange Ideas Ⓒ James Strange

5A Ⓓ Jedzkolor Ⓒ Freak Studio Poznan 5B Ⓓ Lucero Design Ⓒ Bernalillo High School 5C Ⓓ Distillery Design Studio Ⓒ American Library Association 5D Ⓓ Gyula Nemeth Ⓒ Budapest Film

Art Gallery of Alberta
Identity Design

Vision Creative, Edmonton, Alberta, Canada

In late 2009, after months of developing a brand strategy for the gallery, Vision Creative designed a new identity for the Art Gallery of Alberta. The gallery's old building, located in the center of Edmonton's Arts District, was demolished, and an extraordinary new building went up in its footprint. The new structure signaled the ideal moment to reintroduce the gallery and a new experience to the populace.

"Many people have lived here for years, but have never stepped inside. The gallery wanted to build membership outside of the traditional core audience, which was small," explains Vision Creative art director and partner, Brad Blasko. The new building and new identity could serve together to reintroduce this community asset to everyone.

Above: The new Art Gallery of Alberta (Photo: Robert Lemermeyer)

Above center: The AGA logo encourages the viewer to take a second look, just as the gallery developers wanted Alberta citizens to take a fresh look at art and the facility.

The building has a rather fantastic shape. Designed by Randall Stout Architects, it is crowned with an enormous ribbon of twisting, undulating steel meant to represent both the aurora borealis and the city's winding North Saskatchewan River. It is a structure that clearly has a personality of its own.

Blasko's team was, at the same time, challenged and inspired by the structure. They wanted to play into the building's shape, but not so much as to overwhelm.

"There are many waves and curves in the architecture. The new identity, though, does need to be somewhat case-neutral to the building. We couldn't go too modern, because this is not a modern gallery. It is the province's gallery, with a mandate to exhibit many forms of art," Blasko says. Lowercase Helvetica, he explains, was an excellent, case-neutral choice. "Helvetica is a classic face that has stood the test of time. It is not specific to an era."

The designers' solution utilizes a single letter *a* and simply repeats its shape. The *a* used as a *g* is clearly readable, but the flip provides a visual and creative twist that speaks to the art gallery's core purpose. Overlapping the shapes connected them, which Blasko says relates the gallery connecting to the community—the primary component of the new brand promise.

The palette comes from colors in the aurora borealis: It includes green, red, orange, blue, purple, and a cool gray. The colors are translucent, allowing the letter shapes to play off of each other and create new tones.

Blasko says he likes the typographic play. It subtly represents the artistic process.

"It's the simplest of shapes and reads well large or small. It plays well off of a core thought: Look at art again. It changes perception, which I like," Blasko says.

LOGO SEARCH

Keywords: **Birds**

Type: ◯ Symbol ◯ Typographic ◯ Combo ◉ All

A **B** **C** **D**

1

2

3

4

5

Ⓓ = Design Firm Ⓒ = Client

1C Ⓓ Kuznetsov Evgeniy | KUZNETS Ⓒ Kuznetsov Evgeniy 1D Ⓓ Glitschka Studios Ⓒ Brett St.Amour

2A Ⓓ Gardner Design Ⓒ Phoenix Productions 2B Ⓓ Archrival Ⓒ Academy of Rock 2C Ⓓ Draward Ⓒ MW 2D Ⓓ Fargo Design Co., Inc. Ⓒ PA Council Against the Drink Tax

3A Ⓓ Gardner Design Ⓒ Johnathan Goodwin 3B Ⓓ Lippincott Ⓒ UniGroup 3C Ⓓ Lippincott Ⓒ TACA Airlines 3D Ⓓ GeniusLogo Ⓒ sky

4A Ⓓ Fitch Seattle Ⓒ Page Plus Cellular 4B Ⓓ Karl Design Vienna Ⓒ Bildungszentrum Wien 4C Ⓓ Roy Smith Design Ⓒ Roy Smith 4D Ⓓ Gardner Design Ⓒ Kansas Health Ethics

5A Ⓓ A3 Design Ⓒ American Falconry Conservatory 5B Ⓓ Gobranding.eu Ⓒ European Solidarity Center 5C Ⓓ Evenson Design Group Ⓒ St. Vincent Medical Center 5D Ⓓ Clockwork Studios Ⓒ Gethsemane Partners

	A	B	C	D
1				
2				
3				
4				
5				

ⅅ = Design Firm   Ⅽ = Client

1A ⅅ Yatta Yatta Yatta Ⅽ Nuthatch Yarn Works   1B ⅅ Porch Creative ⅭPorch Creative   1C ⅅ TOKY Branding+Design ⅭDavid Bailey   1D ⅅ Ray Dugas Design ⅭRay Dugas Design

2A ⅅ Roger Oddone Design Studio ⅭTaiama   2B ⅅ Sean Heisler ⅭSean Heisler   2C ⅅ Strange Ideas ⅭJames Strange   2D ⅅ Marketsplash by HP ⅭCarmita Products

3A ⅅ creative space ⅭRise and Shine Bakery   3B ⅅ Stebbings Partners ⅭMission Oak Grill   3C ⅅ Diann Cage Design ⅭBluebird Publishing Company   3D ⅅ Gardner Design ⅭMend Physiotherapy

4A ⅅ X3 Studios ⅭPersonal   4B ⅅ supersoon good design ⅭRenate Heyer   4C ⅅ dale harris ⅭLittle Bangs   4D ⅅ Blue Clover ⅭBlue Clover

5A ⅅ Caliber Creative, LLC ⅭCaliber Creative   5B ⅅ Combustion ⅭIndie Memphis   5C ⅅ Alphabet Arm Design ⅭLisa Rigby   5D ⅅ The Action Designer ⅭPersonal Project

	A	B	C	D
1				
2				
3				
4				
5				

D = Design Firm   C = Client

1A D Bertz Design Group C unused   1B D ZORRAQUINO C Gobierno Vasco   1C D TomJon Design Co. C CTT   1D D Newhouse Design C Double Happiness Interior Design

2A D Kindred Design Studio, Inc. C Sterling Construction   2B D www.macamecanica.com C Comtributo Lda.   2C D Judson Design C Cradle Robbers   2D D Gardner Design C Graphic Impressions

3A D IF marketing & advertising C IF marketing & advvertising   3B D Nastasha Beatty Designs C Student Work   3C D Chris Rooney Illustration/Design C Daily Food Company   3D D Tetro Design Incorporated C Prairie Theatre Exchange

4A D Chris Rooney Illustration/Design C Daily Food Company   4B D Rudy Hurtado Global Branding C Chicos Chicken   4C D A3 Design C A3 design   4D D RedBrand C RusPole

5A D Dotzero Design C Falcon Art Community   5B D Dotzero Design C Falcon Art Community   5C D Gardner Design C Phoenix Productions   5D D Gardner Design C Phoenix Productions

A	B	C	D	
 STORCHEN APOTHEKE TIENGEN	 CHARLESTON NATURALLY	 Motherhood Later ...THAN SOONER		1
 ugly duck.	 IRON DUCK clothing	 CANADIAN SWAN		2
 SCHWANEN apotheke				3
	 the PINGWINS TABLE TENNIS TEAM	 hatchcrm		4
	Point Reyes Birding & Nature Festival		elefly	5

Ⓓ = Design Firm   Ⓒ = Client

1A Ⓓ Kommunikation & Design Ⓒ Storchen Apotheke Tiengen 1B Ⓓ J Fletcher Design Ⓒ Charleston Naturally 1C Ⓓ creative space Ⓒ Motherhood Later 1D Ⓓ insight design Ⓒ South Texas Surfacing

2A Ⓓ X3 Studios Ⓒ Ugly Duck 2B Ⓓ Siah Design Ⓒ Siah Design 2C Ⓓ mIQelangelo Ⓒ Canada 2D Ⓓ Sabingrafik, Inc. Ⓒ Hotel Bel-Air

3A Ⓓ Karl Design Vienna Ⓒ Karl Design 3B Ⓓ Univisual Ⓒ Loretoprint 3C Ⓓ Steve Cantrell Ⓒ Escape Bahamas 3D Ⓓ Johnston Duffy Ⓒ OKI Data America

4A Ⓓ MINE Ⓒ MINE 4B Ⓓ Jason Kirshenblatt Ⓒ Pingwins Table Tennis Team 4C Ⓓ IF marketing & advertising Ⓒ IF marketing & advertising 4D Ⓓ ballard::creative Ⓒ Gaylord Texan Resort

5A Ⓓ Todd Linkner Design Associates Ⓒ Todd Linkner Design Associates 5B Ⓓ Deutsch Design Works Ⓒ Environmental Action Committee West Marin 5C Ⓓ Bronson Ma Creative Ⓒ Fire Action Pros 5D Ⓓ Logoguppy Ⓒ elefly

LOGO SEARCH

Keywords **Fish, Bugs, Reptiles**

Type: ◯ Symbol ◯ Typographic ◯ Combo ⦿ All

Ⓓ = Design Firm   Ⓒ = Client

1C Ⓓ Roy Smith Design Ⓒ Fortuna   1D Ⓓ Jason Drumheller Ⓒ Downtown Partnership of Baltimore

2A Ⓓ Logorado Ⓒ Bigcolors   2B Ⓓ Marketsplash by HP Ⓒ Bass Girl   2C Ⓓ The Modern Brand Company Ⓒ Dyron's Lowcountry Restaurant   2D Ⓓ Elevation Creative Studios Ⓒ Whisker's Restaurant & Tavern

3A Ⓓ RetroMetro Designs Ⓒ rockfish group   3B Ⓓ Roskelly Inc. Ⓒ Fish Market Koper Slovenia   3C Ⓓ Jan Sabach Design Ⓒ Perfect Crowd   3D Ⓓ GeniusLogo Ⓒ fish line

4A Ⓓ Romulo Moya / Trama Ⓒ Pillon Pesca   4B Ⓓ Sabin Design Ⓒ Pacific Seafood Group   4C Ⓓ Karl Design Vienna Ⓒ Druckerei Fischer Wien   4D Ⓓ Fresh Creative Ⓒ Seribu Rasa

5A Ⓓ alekchmura.com Ⓒ Alek Chmura   5B Ⓓ interbrand Ⓒ Seattle Children's Hospital   5C Ⓓ Yury Akulin | Logodiver Ⓒ Logodiver   5D Ⓓ Siah Design Ⓒ Undersea Productions

	A	B	C	D	

    **1**

   **2**

    **3**

    **4**

    **5**

ⓓ = Design Firm   ⓒ = Client

1A ⓓ petervasvari.com ⓒ petervasvari.com 1B ⓓ Creative Beard ⓒ Chris Taylor 1C ⓓ Mongoose - The Web Company ⓒ Shoal Creek Beer&Bugs 1D ⓓ Logoguppy ⓒ crabloft

2A ⓓ Felixsockwell.com ⓒ cbs 2B ⓓ dee duncan ⓒ squid ink creative 2C ⓓ Gobranding.eu ⓒ PUMS 2D ⓓ Tran Creative ⓒ Venom

3A ⓓ Karl Design Vienna ⓒ Karl Design Vienna 3B ⓓ Caliber Creative, LLC ⓒ XTO Energy 3C ⓓ Hazen Creative, Inc. ⓒ TurtleScarf/Allay California 3D ⓓ Fumiko Noon ⓒ Fumiko Noon

4A ⓓ Strange Ideas ⓒ James Strange 4B ⓓ Michael Spitz ⓒ Michael Spitz 4C ⓓ Michael Spitz ⓒ Michael Spitz 4D ⓓ Gardner Design ⓒ JumpStartle

5A ⓓ Rico Maier Communication Design (B.A) ⓒ Chameleon Kids Fashion 5B ⓓ Gardner Design ⓒ Graphic Impressions 5C ⓓ Device ⓒ Rian Hughes 5D ⓓ Studio Rayolux ⓒ Jurassic Parliament

	A	B	C	D
1				
2				
3				
4				
5				

Ⓓ = Design Firm **Ⓒ** = Client

1A Ⓓ ten:pm media Ⓒ Advanced Armament Corp. 1B Ⓓ Yury Akulin | Logodiver Ⓒ Comfort Optics 1C Ⓓ Design Invasion Ⓒ Metamorphosis Beauty Studio 1D Ⓓ Empax Ⓒ Matan

2A Ⓓ Judson Design Ⓒ Amerex Energy services 2B Ⓓ Strange Ideas Ⓒ James Strange 2C Ⓓ Roy Smith Design Ⓒ Roy Smith 2D Ⓓ kommunikativ Ⓒ charity lottery Fritz-Winter-school

3A Ⓓ Gardner Design Ⓒ Mend Physiotherapy 3B Ⓓ Roy Smith Design Ⓒ NCC 3C Ⓓ Logoguppy Ⓒ savant 3D Ⓓ Sebastiany Branding & Design Ⓒ Primia

4A Ⓓ Gardner Design Ⓒ Complete Landscaping Systems 4B Ⓓ Strange Ideas Ⓒ James Strange 4C Ⓓ RARE Design Ⓒ personal 4D Ⓓ Rickabaugh Graphics Ⓒ Bee Junk Free

5A Ⓓ Glitschka Studios Ⓒ LightStream Animation 5B Ⓓ julian peck Ⓒ Julian Peck 5C Ⓓ Steve Davis Design Ⓒ TransEnterix 5D Ⓓ Incey Wincey Ⓒ Self

Neolab
Identity Redesign

IlovarStritar, Ljubljana, Slovenia

An open-minded client is a designer's dream. Such was the case for Neolab, a recent client for IlovarStritar, a design office in Ljubljana, Slovenia. Because it consistently seeks new approaches in its IT work, client Neolab wanted a completely revolutionary identity as well.

Neolab is an IT company that specializes in building and connecting business information systems, web applications, and websites. Because the client creates and connects new web environments, IlovarStritar principal Robert Ilovar, co-owner of the studio together with Jernej Stritar, says it made sense to create an identity that imitated an open, developing system.

Like many companies, Neolab had many attributes that it wanted to stress—innovation, accessibility, confidence, creativity, and flexibility, to name a few. Instead of portraying these concepts abstractly, Ilovar decided to represent them literally through a system that possessed the same qualities.

"There are currently about twelve motifs that are used on all visual communications for the company. Each motif is based on a specific meaning, such as the image of a pigeon combined with a

cheetah to indicate postal service and speed. A combined kangaroo and pelican are used on vehicles, as both animals can carry things," he explains.

On the letterhead and invoice there are different dogs, both presenting trust, confidence, and loyalty. On the letterhead, there is a dog combined with a parrot, which stands for communication. On the invoice, there is a dog combined with an owl—intelligence and accuracy.

The main two animals, which are used on the covers of their publications, are a fluffy, white penguin-sheep and a black, furry peacock-mammal. They are both round, with short legs. They seem charming and friendly, and are certainly innovative.

Instead of just melding the animals, though, Ilovar also added another transformation: Each new animal dissolves into pixels from right to left, which relates to the client's online operations. Every new, unique creature can be used as a variable logo next to the Neolab wordmark.

The designer carried the idea onto the company's business cards as well. "On the cards, we blended three animals: one that shows how the employee is perceived by coworkers, one that shows how the employee perceives himself, and one that is actually related to him, say, through his zodiac sign," Ilovar says. The results are as strange as they are memorable.

When the employees saw their pictures, they were enthusiastic. They have adopted their animals and some of them even use their personal animal for their Facebook profile picture.

"Because the client was open-minded and they try to develop new approaches in their field of work, we went beyond the clichés of a visual identity for an IT company," says Ilovar.

	A	B	C	D
1	## LOGO SEARCH Keywords `Animals` Type: ○ Symbol ○ Typographic ○ Combo ● All			
2				
3				
4				
5				

ⅅ = Design Firm   ⅭⅭ = Client

1C ⅅ Michael Spitz ⒸMichael Spitz   1D ⅅ Genaro Solis Ⓒ stay dog hotel (unused)

2A ⅅ Michael Spitz Ⓒ Buzzdog Group   2B ⅅ 5Seven Ⓒ Duboce Park   2C ⅅ SGNL Studio Ⓒ Jeremy Garder   2D ⅅ The Netmen Corp Ⓒ Wi - Fido

3A ⅅ pricedyment Ⓒ 7th Engine   3B ⅅ Chad Mjos Ⓒ Greater Tulsa Veterinary Services   3C ⅅ Sean Heisler Ⓒ Blue Dog Properties   3D ⅅ PUSH Branding and Design Ⓒ BirdDog Jobs

4A ⅅ Design Army Ⓒ Lucky Dog Films   4B ⅅ FORM Ⓒ FIDO (Fully Integrated Desktop Objects)   4C ⅅ Jackrabbit Design Ⓒ Tail Chaser Photography   4D ⅅ Rachel Castor Ⓒ The Dog Hair: Pet Grooming

5A ⅅ Hibblen Design Ⓒ Toedogg Threads   5B ⅅ Imadesign, Corp. Ⓒ Brandkey   5C ⅅ Tomasz Politanski Design Ⓒ Dog Spot   5D ⅅ Riggs Partners Ⓒ Palmetto Animal Assisted Life Services

A	B	C	D	
				1
				2
				3
				4
				5

Ⓓ = Design Firm   Ⓒ = Client

1A Ⓓ wierhouse Ⓒ Pendleton King Park 1B Ⓓ Clashmore Ⓒ Andrew Rozell Photography 1C Ⓓ Riley Designs Ⓒ Noodle the Toodle 1D Ⓓ STUBBORN SIDEBURN Ⓒ House of sarcasm

2A Ⓓ Ross Clodfelter Design Ⓒ Ruff Housing Doggi Daycare 2B Ⓓ Tran Creative Ⓒ DogKennelsandCrates.com 2C Ⓓ Naughtyfish Ⓒ Studio Paws Pet Styling 2D Ⓓ Sussner Design Company Ⓒ Animal Humane Society

3A Ⓓ Gardner Design Ⓒ JumpStartle 3B Ⓓ Graphic design studio by Yurko Gutsulyak Ⓒ Epiffani 3C Ⓓ Device Ⓒ Rian Hughes 3D Ⓓ Chris Rooney Illustration/Design Ⓒ NoLa Advocats

4A Ⓓ Wizemark Ⓒ Unused 4B Ⓓ Trapeze Ⓒ Fairmont Empress 4C Ⓓ Skye Design Studios Ⓒ Methodist University 4D Ⓓ Emilio Correa Ⓒ ARTEIS

5A Ⓓ Pavone Ⓒ Epic Technology 5B Ⓓ Paradox Box Ⓒ Rinat Tuhvatullin 5C Ⓓ Gardner Design Ⓒ Graphic Impressions 5D Ⓓ BrandWell Creative Ⓒ Seven Lions Investments

	A	B	C	D
1				
2				
3				
4				
5				

D = Design Firm   C = Client

1A D Sebastiany Branding & Design C COPEL   1B D Murillo Design, Inc. C Shannon Livingston Companies   1C D Banowetz + Company, Inc. C Androvett Legal Media & Marketing   1D D Glitschka Studios C St. Martins Press

2A D Sean Heisler C Braviant   2B D Yury Akulin | Logodiver C Safari Park   2C D RARE Design C Personal   2D D Gardner Design C The Independent School

3A D Eben Design C Yarmuth Farm Cheese   3B D Tactical Magic C Utopia Animal Hospital   3C D 3x4 Design Studio C Kanoon Co.   3D D Device C RIAN HUGHES

4A D Noble C Noble   4B D Peter Gale Graphic Design C Peter Gale   4C D KW43 BRANDDESIGN C RTI Sports GmbH   4D D DesignPoint, Inc. C California Trophy Hunts

5A D Logo Design Works C Kelly J   5B D Michael Nagy C Michael Nagy   5C D Kastelov C icebuck   5D D Turnpost C Stuart Lundgren

	A	B	C	D
1				
2				
3				
4				
5				

Ⓓ = Design Firm   Ⓒ = Client

1A Ⓓ Ph.D Ⓒ Christmas Run   1B Ⓓ Yatta Yatta Yatta Ⓒ Backcountry Coffee Roasters   1C Ⓓ petervasvari.com Ⓒ Brandstack   1D Ⓓ Tetro Design Incorporated Ⓒ Committee on the Status of Endangered Wildlife in Canada

2A Ⓓ moosylvania Ⓒ Moosylvania   2B Ⓓ the Queen City Studio Ⓒ Okapi   2C Ⓓ Ghiath Lahham Ⓒ Jumeirah   2D Ⓓ Schwartzrock Graphic Arts Ⓒ Design Center

3A Ⓓ Murillo Design, Inc. Ⓒ Shannon Livingston Companies   3B Ⓓ NOT A CANNED HAM Ⓒ Skylab-B Communications   3C Ⓓ Primarily Rye LLC Ⓒ Curtiswood Farms   3D Ⓓ Marketsplash by HP Ⓒ Harvest Moon Market

4A Ⓓ Red Clover Studio Ⓒ Airtex Design Group   4B Ⓓ Schwartzrock Graphic Arts Ⓒ Design Center   4C Ⓓ Najlon Ⓒ KADAR 22   4D Ⓓ Koodoz Design Ⓒ Tullamore Estate

5A Ⓓ Strange Ideas Ⓒ James Strange   5B Ⓓ The Design Engine, LLC Ⓒ Video Wisconsin   5C Ⓓ Razor Creative Ⓒ Jeff Hughes   5D Ⓓ Oxide Design Co. Ⓒ Silicon Prairie News

	A	B	C	D
1				
2				
3				
4				
5				

D = Design Firm   C = Client

1A Ⓓ Graphismo Ⓒ The Williamson Museum   1B Ⓓ ab designwerks Ⓒ El Toothpick   1C Ⓓ SEMAFOR Ⓒ Bank PEKAO SA   1D Ⓓ Logoguppy Ⓒ AquaBull

2A Ⓓ Gardner Design Ⓒ Trails Crossing   2B Ⓓ Logoguppy Ⓒ Bullify   2C Ⓓ Indicia Design Inc Ⓒ Koala Kuddles   2D Ⓓ Worth | Design Ⓒ Arizona Science Center

3A Ⓓ Cooper Smith and Company Ⓒ Standard Bearings   3B Ⓓ Sabingrafik, Inc. Ⓒ Seafarer Baking Company   3C Ⓓ Glitschka Studios Ⓒ Landor Associates   3D Ⓓ Sabingrafik, Inc. Ⓒ San Diego Zoo

4A Ⓓ Sabingrafik, Inc. Ⓒ San Diego Zoo   4B Ⓓ Sabingrafik, Inc. Ⓒ San Diego Zoo   4C Ⓓ Tannehill Design Ⓒ Bayer Protective Services   4D Ⓓ Suprematika Ⓒ Rucksack

5A Ⓓ Headwerk Ⓒ Bunny Jones   5B Ⓓ Strange Ideas Ⓒ James Strange   5C Ⓓ Noriu Menulio (Current) Ⓒ Tie Kepejai   5D Ⓓ Incitrio Ⓒ Shorthand Mobile

	A	B	C	D
1	 SKUNK LAND	 BRat	 roorag	
2		 ELEPHANT BAR		
3	 REPUBLICANS FOR RAPE	 urban thai	 UNION	 CSS-GROUP
4	 KEBET CORRUGATED CARTONS			
5			 CONSUMMATE PET	

Ⓓ = Design Firm   Ⓒ = Client

1A Ⓓ Strange Ideas Ⓒ James Strange   1B Ⓓ Device Ⓒ MILLION DOLLAR   1C Ⓓ Gizwiz Studio Ⓒ Chuah Shue Ping   1D Ⓓ Paradox Box Ⓒ Rinat Tuhvatullin

2A Ⓓ eight a.m. brand design (shanghai) Co., Ltd Ⓒ aile-ideer brand   2B Ⓓ Keo Pierron Ⓒ Elephant Bar   2C Ⓓ Home Grown Logos Ⓒ Empower Your Shower   2D Ⓓ Gardner Design Ⓒ Leaf Patrol

3A Ⓓ Steven O'Connor Ⓒ RepublicansForRape.org   3B Ⓓ XY ARTS Ⓒ Urban Thai   3C Ⓓ onetreeink Ⓒ Union inc.   3D Ⓓ Cheltsov Ⓒ CSS-GROUP

4A Ⓓ Peter Gale Graphic Design Ⓒ Peter Gale   4B Ⓓ Blacktop Creative Ⓒ MySpace   4C Ⓓ Visualism Ⓒ visualism   4D Ⓓ Gardner Design Ⓒ Ecommerce Mechanics

5A Ⓓ Heisel Design Ⓒ Brand Monkey   5B Ⓓ Strange Ideas Ⓒ James Strange   5C Ⓓ The Greater Good Design Ⓒ Consummate Pet   5D Ⓓ Infestation Ⓒ Champions of the Environment Foundation

Pula
Identity Design

Parabureau, Zagreb, Croatia

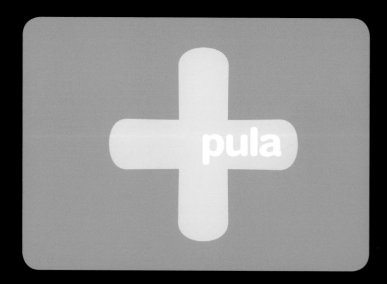

In considering Pula's many attractions, they came up with the slogan, "Pula is More." The word more made them see the yellow cross in a new way: as a plus sign.

"The old emblem and its green and yellow colors were already widely accepted by Pula's inhabitants, so we used it as the basis for the visual identity," says art director Igor Stanisljevic. "The Latin cross from the emblem was transformed into the plus sign." Now the equation could be almost anything: Pula + whatever the city wanted to promote.

The designers also created a modular visual communications system which visually depicts various combinations, such as "concert + amphitheater," or "beach life + cultural event." The intriguing combinations of visuals made citizens and tourists alike take a new look at Pula.

The design team selected lowercase letters in Heisei Maru Gothic for several reasons: First, this face in the lowercase was a good compositional balance with the plus sign. The other reason was more hidden, but it makes sense for a city that wants to appear to be more contemporary: "We wanted to move away from Roman capitals," says Stanisljevic.

It's not every day that a design firm is approached by a 2,000-year-old client. That explains, in part, Parabureau's very modern yet very traditional identity solution for the Croatian city of Pula.

Pula is the largest city in Istria County, Croatia, situated at the southern tip of the Istria Peninsula. The Pula City Tourist Board asked Parabureau (Zagreb) to create a visual identity that would better promote the city to tourists. Its existing crest was a traditionally flavored emblem that contained a bold yellow Latin cross set on a green coat-of-arms shield. It was not very twenty-first-century in its old manifestation, but the Parabureau designers saw a lot of potential in keeping the cross.

Creative/art directors: Igor Stanisljevic and Marko Baus
Strategists: Igor Stanisljevic and Marko Baus
Art director: Petar Popovic
Designers: Maja Turcic, Kristina Ivancic

The new Pula city logo with a variety of applications that demonstrate the "plus" concept behind the design.

LOGO SEARCH

Keywords **Nature**

Type: ○ Symbol   ○ Typographic   ○ Combo   ● All

CANADA

CANADIANATIVE

CANADIAN
MISSIONS
INITIATIVE

Accellion
GREEN

RIVER OAKS

DOCK WOODS
A LIVING BRANCHES COMMUNITY

CHILDREN'S
ENVIRONMENTAL HEALTH INSTITUTE

ecotouch™

edible
SUSTAINABLE
GARDENING

GLENORA

Grow
Native
every drop matters.

ⓓ = Design Firm   ⓒ = Client

1C ⓓ Niedermeier Design ⓒ Clear Bags   1D ⓓ Brand Agent ⓒ Unused

2A ⓓ Logo Design Works ⓒ Canadian Golf Links   2B ⓓ Thomas Cook Designs ⓒ Canadian Missions Initiative   2C ⓓ Landkamer Partners, Inc. ⓒ Landkamer Partners   2D ⓓ A.D. Creative Group ⓒ Oakland Home Builders Corp.

3A ⓓ Pavone ⓒ Living Branches   3B ⓓ PurEthanol ⓒ Children's Environmental Health Institute   3C ⓓ Du4 Designs ⓒ Applied Solar Inc.   3D ⓓ Kolar Advertising and Marketing ⓒ AgVenture Travel

4A ⓓ Blue Tricycle, Inc. ⓒ The Content Crafters   4B ⓓ jo ⓒ Numas Sustainability   4C ⓓ artslinger ⓒ Glenora Community   4D ⓓ Studio Grafik ⓒ Shin Ryoku

5A ⓓ ADC Global Creativity ⓒ Lake Arrowhead Community Services District   5B ⓓ TOKY Branding+Design ⓒ Brochsteins Woodworking   5C ⓓ Deney ⓒ Kamed   5D ⓓ KENNETH DISENO ⓒ RICO Y NATURAL

	A	B	C	D
1				
2				
3				
4				
5				

 = Design Firm   © = Client

1A Ⓓ eight a.m. brand design (shanghai) Co., Ltd Ⓒ laichy   1B Ⓓ LeBoYe Ⓒ kayumanis boutique villas   1C Ⓓ julian peck Ⓒ Sea Change   1D Ⓓ Six17 Ⓒ Mel Campbell

2A Ⓓ Aars | Wells Ⓒ InnerChange   2B Ⓓ Studio Ink Ⓒ Crusoe College   2C Ⓓ PenPixel Design Ⓒ PenPixel Design   2D Ⓓ Schwartzrock Graphic Arts Ⓒ Erica Allen

3A Ⓓ Studio Hill Design Ⓒ By The Yard   3B Ⓓ Caliber Creative, LLC Ⓒ Northwest Bible Church   3C Ⓓ X3 Studios Ⓒ Seed Fund Management   3D Ⓓ ORFIK DESIGN Ⓒ Plakias Resorts & Properties

4A Ⓓ Sebastiany Branding & Design Ⓒ Fazenda do Braco do Eta   4B Ⓓ Luke Baker Ⓒ Enough to Spare   4C Ⓓ Studio 2108 Ⓒ St. Louis Composting   4D Ⓓ Sebastiany Branding & Design Ⓒ Ecolabor

5A Ⓓ LeBoYe Ⓒ The Royale Springhill   5B Ⓓ Artisticodopeo Designz Ⓒ The Blue Lotus   5C Ⓓ TOMCOM, Konzeption und Gestaltung Ⓒ MANA Verlag   5D Ⓓ Webster Design Associates Inc. Ⓒ United Nations

	A	B	C	D

1

2

3

4

5

ⒹＤ = Design Firm   ⒸＣ = Client

1A Ⓓ moosylvania Ⓒ Aqualok   1B Ⓓ Sauvage Design Ⓒ Discover Health   1C Ⓓ Ryan Miller Design Ⓒ Nature Scape Management   1D Ⓓ Juan Pablo Tredicce Ⓒ Juan Pablo Tredicce

2A Ⓓ josh higgins design Ⓒ Vijolance   2B Ⓓ Karl Design Vienna Ⓒ Lujong Eva Furrer   2C Ⓓ Dalius Stuoka Ⓒ Demiu   2D Ⓓ M10 Design Ⓒ Sindfhort-DF

3A Ⓓ Elements Ⓒ Tienshan   3B Ⓓ Tom Hughes Ⓒ Energy Innovations / Idealab   3C Ⓓ IF marketing & advertising Ⓒ groovy spoon   3D Ⓓ mlsane industries Ⓒ Triangle Women's Lacrosse

4A Ⓓ Jolt Ⓒ Dandelion   4B Ⓓ The Pink Pear Design Company Ⓒ Dandelion Pages   4C Ⓓ Boswell Design Solutions Ⓒ Nevada Cancer Institute   4D Ⓓ Carve Ⓒ Idlewyld Inn

5A Ⓓ planet of shapes Ⓒ MRU 2025   5B Ⓓ Helikopter Reklambyra Ⓒ Vasterbottens Kakelugnsmakeri   5C Ⓓ Gavula Design Associates Ⓒ The Fund for Public Schools   5D Ⓓ BrandBerry Ⓒ ZipCoin

	A	**B**	**C**	**D**
1				
2				
3				
4				
5				

Ⓓ = Design Firm   Ⓒ = Client

1A Ⓓ Strange Ideas Ⓒ James Strange   1B Ⓓ Christopher Dina Ⓒ City of Tokigawa (Proposed)   1C Ⓓ D&i (Design and Image) Ⓒ Ryan Cooper   1D Ⓓ huebner petersen Ⓒ Instructional Coaching Group

2A Ⓓ Stitch Design Co. Ⓒ Anne Bowen   2B Ⓓ Sudduth Design Co. Ⓒ St. John's United Methodist   2C Ⓓ keith cummings Ⓒ green thumb   2D Ⓓ Orange Label Ⓒ Droits de l'Homme en Asie Centrale

3A Ⓓ Dreambox Creative Ⓒ Liquid Bamboo   3B Ⓓ Sabingrafik, Inc. Ⓒ San Diego International Airport   3C Ⓓ ID.Brand Ⓒ Sumatra Palm Industry   3D Ⓓ brandStrata Ⓒ Desert Teak

4A Ⓓ Jeffhalmos Ⓒ Treefrog   4B Ⓓ Hvita husid Ⓒ Krikaskóli   4C Ⓓ 01d Ⓒ bouqet.ru   4D Ⓓ Ramp Ⓒ UCLA

5A Ⓓ Bronson Ma Creative Ⓒ Hostess Brands   5B Ⓓ Jeremy Slagle Design Ⓒ Justice Gardens   5C Ⓓ Mattson Creative Ⓒ Brilliant Sky   5D Ⓓ Mattson Creative Ⓒ Brilliant Sky

A	B	C	D	
		 **Seaport Sustainability** Symposium	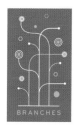 BRANCHES	1
		 gonorth		2
	 STRATEGICO	 ELPASO**FOUNDATION**	 **WILDER**	3
 **ANCHORPOINT** CHRISTIAN SCHOOL		 AiCM	 Chester Springs Surrounds natural charm.	4
	 MA TERRE	 OLEY SPRINGS FARM	 BARTLETT ARBORETUM 100 YEARS	5

Ⓓ = Design Firm   Ⓒ = Client

1A Ⓓ Majorminor Ⓒ Happy Little Tree Clothing 1B Ⓓ Bozell Ⓒ TownCommons.com 1C Ⓓ Hubbell Design Works Ⓒ Port of Long Beach 1D Ⓓ Mattson Creative Ⓒ Branches

2A Ⓓ Diva Design Ⓒ Wisdom Years 2B Ⓓ Gardner Design Ⓒ Books for Life 2C Ⓓ Christopher Labno Ⓒ GoNorth 2D Ⓓ BrandBerry Ⓒ cManager

3A Ⓓ Gardner Design Ⓒ Kansas Health Ethics 3B Ⓓ Naughtyfish Ⓒ Strategico 3C Ⓓ VIVA Creative Group Ⓒ El Paso Foundation 3D Ⓓ Sockeye Creative Ⓒ Landwaves

4A Ⓓ Deksia Ⓒ AnchorPoint Christian School 4B Ⓓ RADAR Agency Ⓒ The Live Oak Institute 4C Ⓓ Tran Creative Ⓒ American Institute of Clinical Massage 4D Ⓓ Caspari McCormick Ⓒ Leila Marvel

5A Ⓓ Sabingrafik, Inc. Ⓒ Rosenblum Cellars 5B Ⓓ Watel Design Ⓒ Ma Terre 5C Ⓓ Marlin Ⓒ Oley Springs Farm 5D Ⓓ Gardner Design Ⓒ Bartlett Arboretum

	A	B	C	D
1				
2				
3				
4	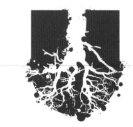			
5				

ⓓ = Design Firm   ⓒ = Client

1A ⓓ C7 Design ⓒ Thrive Food Coaching   1B ⓓ LeBoYe ⓒ Blessed Community   1C ⓓ Bernas Design ⓒ Frank Bernas   1D ⓓ Small Dog Design ⓒ Tree House Domaine

2A ⓓ Franke+Fiorella ⓒ Orchard Dental Group   2B ⓓ For the Love of Creating ⓒ Woods Orthodontic Arts   2C ⓓ AT PACE ⓒ Tortilis Africa   2D ⓓ TypeOrange ⓒ Oliva

3A ⓓ Red Clover Studio ⓒ Airtex Design Group   3B ⓓ Timber Design Company ⓒ 8Fifteen   3C ⓓ Rpd Design ⓒ Acapi - Beekeeping   3D ⓓ Limelight Advertising & Design ⓒ Forest Windows

4A ⓓ The Martin Group ⓒ Renovation Church   4B ⓓ Luke Despatie & The Design Firm ⓒ Oak Heights   4C ⓓ Juicebox Designs ⓒ Treehouse Records   4D ⓓ PUSH Branding and Design ⓒ Agrinuity

5A ⓓ KROG, d.o.o. ⓒ Pomurski sejem, Gornja Radgona   5B ⓓ bartodell.com ⓒ Attebury Grain Inc.   5C ⓓ 903 Creative, LLC ⓒ Park Group   5D ⓓ Mary Hutchison Design LLC ⓒ Smart Chocolate LLC

	A	B	C	D	
1	 TRINCHERO *Family Wines*	 Whisperwood at Wing Point	 tuscany	 PIEDMONT BANK	1
2	 RIVERGLEN NATURE'S GOLF COURSE	 PEAKS 2 PRAIRIE		 Water Empire	2
3	reSnow	 cinnia édua FASHION & ART GALLERY	LULLABY STUDIO		3
4				PHOENIX ORIGINALS	4
5	 SAINT GERMAIN CATERING	 PHOENIX GALLERIA			5
6					

Ⓓ = Design Firm   Ⓒ = Client

1A Ⓓ Sabingrafik, Inc. Ⓒ Trinchero Family Wines   1B Ⓓ William Herod Design Ⓒ Whisperwood at Wing Point   1C Ⓓ Kelley Nixon Ⓒ Kelley Nixon   1D Ⓓ Matchstic Ⓒ Piedmont Bank

2A Ⓓ Miles Design Ⓒ River Glen   2B Ⓓ A.D. Creative Group Ⓒ Peaks to Prairie   2C Ⓓ dbDESIGNS Ⓒ Self   2D Ⓓ Orange Label Ⓒ Weater Empire

3A Ⓓ Wizemark Ⓒ 365 Logo Project   3B Ⓓ Voov Ltd. Ⓒ Cinnia Édua - Klodess Ltd.   3C Ⓓ Almosh82 Ⓒ Lullaby Studio   3D Ⓓ Cooper Design Ⓒ Lunar Mattress

4A Ⓓ Gardner Design Ⓒ Earth Wind Fire Water   4B Ⓓ Derrick Mitchell Design, LLC Ⓒ Easthaven Baptist Church   4C Ⓓ Freight Train Ⓒ The East Side Business Improvement District   4D Ⓓ 3906 Design Ⓒ 3906 Design

5A Ⓓ Red Thinking Ⓒ Saint Germain Catering   5B Ⓓ Hand dizajn studio Ⓒ Phoenix Capitis   5C Ⓓ entz creative Ⓒ DayHater.com   5D Ⓓ GingerBee Creative Ⓒ Big Sky Custom Solar

Ruhland & Ruhland
Identity Start-Up

Jessica Hische, Brooklyn, New York

The Ruhland & Ruhland project is one that illustrates Jessica Hische's belief that referencing is fine—to a point. Slavish repetition of a historical style or overornamentation shows no creativity, and it also reveals a lack of confidence in one's own drawing skills.

Case in point: Felix Ruhland wanted to open a gourmet deli in Germany that would do what delis do most everywhere else—prepare sandwiches and offer foods from around the world. But delis in Germany are something of a rarity, so the identity for his store would have to speak clearly about what a deli is.

He contacted Hische and gave her lots of images for inspiration, mostly ads and packaging examples from the late 1800s and turn of the century in the United States and Europe.

He was looking for something Victorian but not stodgy. The effect needed to be somewhat modern, recalls Hische. He also wanted the store to look like it had been there for a long time, and that it should look neutral—neither overly American nor European.

The designer's thoughts after viewing all of the client's materials were to do two approaches—something script-ish and something more straightforward, both with ornaments that had a vintage feel.

"For the small type, I had already created a lowercase alphabet based on Engraver's Gothic. Engraver's Gothic is a really useful font with a vintage feel that works great as tiny type, but this needed to be a bit quirkier with a bit more of a handcrafted feeling. The alphabet was going to be a very important supporting element for this project," she says.

Hische, who does most of her sketching in Adobe Illustrator, drew skeletons of the type she had in mind and worked from there.

She keeps the final application of the design in mind as she works.

"If it's going to be the size of a billboard, I would go crazy with ornamentation. But this would have to look good on a business card. The process is very addictive. I have to recognize when I'm overworking it," she says. "Over-ornamentation is a way to mask your inability to draw or your ability to set type beautifully. You have to be able to fix those little Illustrator errors, not add more stuff. People forget the purpose of design—to communicate, not to decorate."

The client ultimately selected the all-caps version of Hische's design rather than the script. Hische specified a neutral gold-yellow for the ornament and black for the type, which made for a good neutral vintage color palette while still keeping the type very legible.

Above: Designer Jessica Hische created two possible logo candidates for her German deli client. He selected the Roman version.

LOGO SEARCH

Keywords | **Shapes**

Type: ○ Symbol ○ Typographic ○ Combo ● All

A | B | C | D

aст
research

1

expo
2012

International
Festival of Cultural
Diversity

Consultorías360°

2

 LLOYD
GROSSVERBRAUCHER SERVICE

AMILO   PRIMERGY   FLEXFRAME

3

Indufor

 artemis

URV

4

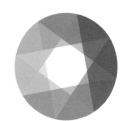

5

ⓓ = Design Firm   ⓒ = Client

1C ⓓ Sakideamsheni ⓒ ACT   1D ⓓ Sakideamsheni ⓒ Expo Georgia

2A ⓓ Sean Heisler ⓒ Ayasdi   2B ⓓ Karl Design Vienna ⓒ Unesco (proposal)   2C ⓓ Gizwiz Studio ⓒ Chuah Shue Ping   2D ⓓ Rise Design Branding Inc. ⓒ CBIN (China Business Information Network)

3A ⓓ Rise Design Branding Inc. ⓒ Higien Medical Inc.   3B ⓓ Sebastiany Branding & Design ⓒ Pepsico   3C ⓓ Braue: Brand Design Experts ⓒ Lloyd Großverbraucher Service GmbH & Co.KG

3D ⓓ KW43 BRANDDESIGN ⓒ Fujitsu Siemens   4A ⓓ Porkka & Kuutsa Oy ⓒ Indufor Oy   4B ⓓ Retro DC ⓒ Artemis   4C ⓓ Porkka & Kuutsa Oy ⓒ URV Oy   4D ⓓ BrandBerry ⓒ Innova Biotechs

5A ⓓ KITA International | Visual Playground ⓒ church congress proposal   5B ⓓ Today ⓒ Proudfield   5C ⓓ Tom Hughes ⓒ Organized Light   5D ⓓ Tom Hughes ⓒ Picasa / Idealab

151

3RD STONE
CONSULTING

CREATIVE
COLLABOS

mystic

karma

bluegreen
paint your world

KARMA
COFFEE

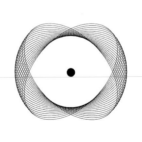

acumeno

joyce miyagishima

VIRTUAL RADIOLOGIC

m | 99

SUNNYSIDE
FEDERAL

ⓓ = Design Firm   ⓒ = Client

1A ⓓ Gardner Design ⓒ Chrysler   1B ⓓ maria guarracino ⓒ gsw worldwide   1C ⓓ Oxide Design Co. ⓒ Quantum Workplace   1D ⓓ Sebastiany Branding & Design ⓒ COPEL

2A ⓓ Niedermeier Design ⓒ Third Stone Consulting   2B ⓓ Axygene ⓒ Creative Collabos   2C ⓓ Phony Lawn ⓒ Young Presidents' Organization   2D ⓓ Ferreira Design Company ⓒ Coca-Cola

3A ⓓ Mattson Creative ⓒ strada Advertising/Hillwood Developments   3B ⓓ Altagraf ⓒ Stack Design   3C ⓓ Almosh82 ⓒ bluegreen   3D ⓓ Tran Creative ⓒ Karma Coffee

4A ⓓ Juan Pablo Tredicce ⓒ Ophthalmology Center / Dr. Jorge L. Tredicce   4B ⓓ ARTENTIKO ⓒ acumeno   4C ⓓ designsgirl ⓒ Joyce Miyagishima   4D ⓓ Chris Herron Design ⓒ Designsite

5A ⓓ W Creative / Brauer Design Co. ⓒ Virtual Radiologic   5B ⓓ noe design ⓒ Mission 99   5C ⓓ Gerren Lamson ⓒ Start Solar   5D ⓓ Visual Language LLC ⓒ Sunnyside Federal Savings and Loan

	A	B	C	D

THE CENTER FOR
TRANSFORMATIVE
LEADERSHIP

 campus living villages

 **1**

ADORA

aldaco

colourys

artesis **2**

COMMUNITY
FOUNDATIONS
OF CANADA

 WINEMOSAIC

YOUR COUNTRY
YOUR CALL  **3**

 C12
Capital Management

INOVAZ™

 **4**

V C A S T

O3GARDEN

MARKITFORCE
On Track On Time **5**

ⓓ = Design Firm   ⓒ = Client

1A ⓓ Taylor Design Works ⓒ Center for Transformative Leadership   1B ⓓ Strategy Design ⓒ Campus Living Villages   1C ⓓ Floris Design ⓒ Inspiral Technology   1D ⓓ Roy Smith Design ⓒ Further

2A ⓓ Andrei Bilan ⓒ Adora Mall   2B ⓓ Eggra ⓒ aldaco   2C ⓓ GeniusLogo ⓒ colourys   2D ⓓ Gramma ⓒ Artesis

3A ⓓ Manifest Communications ⓒ Community Foundations of Canada   3B ⓓ Floris Design ⓒ WineMosaic   3C ⓓ The Brand Hatchery ⓒ Dallas Parks & Recreation   3D ⓓ Neworld Associates ⓒ An Smaoineamh Mor

4A ⓓ Effusion Creative Solutions ⓒ Aasia   4B ⓓ TPG Architecture ⓒ C12 Capital Management   4C ⓓ dache ⓒ David Pache   4D ⓓ Alik Yakubovich agency ⓒ Carcade leasing

5A ⓓ Strange Ideas ⓒ James Strange   5B ⓓ Strange Ideas ⓒ James Strange   5C ⓓ Vlad Ermolaev ⓒ International CIS and Baltia Sports Committee   5D ⓓ DEVELOPED IMAGE PTE LTD ⓒ MarkItForce

	A	B	C	D
1				
2				
3				
4				
5				

Ⓓ = Design Firm   Ⓒ = Client

1A Ⓓ Glitschka Studios Ⓒ Schizo Ltd.   1B Ⓓ Jase Neapolitan Design Ⓒ Students for Humanity   1C Ⓓ 01d Ⓒ Study and Travel   1D Ⓓ EIGHTDAY STUDIO Ⓒ Agent Networking

2A Ⓓ Niedermeier Design Ⓒ Movondo   2B Ⓓ Device Ⓒ Device   2C Ⓓ Majorminor Ⓒ Mase Center @ Sacramento State   2D Ⓓ Pure Fusion Media Ⓒ Team Coop

3A Ⓓ Hayes Image Ⓒ Wild Thorns Motorcycle Club   3B Ⓓ Victor Goloubinov Ⓒ Kifato   3C Ⓓ Jase Neapolitan Design Ⓒ Combined National Campaign   3D Ⓓ RONODESIGN Ⓒ Thailand Population and Housing Cansus

4A Ⓓ The Netmen Corp Ⓒ Captiva   4B Ⓓ Judson Design Ⓒ Israel Aerospace (unused)   4C Ⓓ LogoDesignGuru.com Ⓒ B2it Solutions   4D Ⓓ Wizemark Ⓒ Srdjan Kirtic

5A Ⓓ Synsation Graphic Design Ⓒ Seamless Merchandising Matters   5B Ⓓ Gerren Lamson Ⓒ Local Abounds Charity   5C Ⓓ Jerron Ames Ⓒ Marketsplash   5D Ⓓ LONI DBS Ⓒ Insittute for Humanistic Research in Sport

A **B** **C** **D**

1

 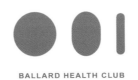 

2

3

PROPERTY
MANAGEMENT
COMPANY
ARCADE

4

5

ⓓ = Design Firm   ⓒ = Client

1A ⓓ Axygene ⓒ OGO   1B ⓓ Device ⓒ Device   1C ⓓ volatile-graphics ⓒ Darren Gordon   1D ⓓ Design & Co ⓒ Kreogene Inc

2A ⓓ dee duncan ⓒ anderson energy   2B ⓓ Niedermeier Design ⓒ Data Analysis   2C ⓓ Strange Ideas ⓒ James Strange   2D ⓓ TriLion Studios ⓒ Brian White

3A ⓓ DNKSTUDIO ⓒ PINTERRA   3B ⓓ Yotam Hadar ⓒ Yotam Hadar   3C ⓓ Mattson Creative ⓒ Mottsy   3D ⓓ Strange Ideas ⓒ James Strange

4A ⓓ Paradox Box ⓒ Property management company ARCADE   4B ⓓ One up ⓒ AFPAR   4C ⓓ Noriu Menulio (Current) ⓒ Silverstone Advisors   4D ⓓ Transformer Studio ⓒ FutureBrand

5A ⓓ BrandBerry ⓒ Olive   5B ⓓ Croak Design ⓒ Expertprint   5C ⓓ Floc5 ⓒ Centree Business   5D ⓓ Kastelov ⓒ movo

Ⓓ = Design Firm ⒸClient

1A Ⓓ Karl Design Vienna Ⓒ Prosoniq GmbH   1B Ⓓ Mattson Creative Ⓒ Mottsy   1C Ⓓ Gramma Ⓒ Flemish Community   1D Ⓓ American Coatings Association Ⓒ American Coatings Association

2A Ⓓ IF marketing & advertising Ⓒ Shawn Ng   2B Ⓓ Anna Kovecses Ⓒ dotsongs   2C Ⓓ ARTENTIKO Ⓒ Seec   2D Ⓓ Ⓒ Siren Design UK

3A Ⓓ Emilio Correa Ⓒ ARTEIS   3B Ⓓ RED The Agency Ⓒ RED The Agency   3C Ⓓ Deney Ⓒ Elara Communication   3D Ⓓ Anthony Lane Studios Ⓒ Lindsay Quinn

4A Ⓓ Zookeeper LLC Ⓒ Benson Marketing Group   4B Ⓓ Kuznetsov Evgeniy | KUZNETS Ⓒ advert media   4C Ⓓ Kuznetsov Evgeniy | KUZNETS Ⓒ Kuznetsov Evgeniy   4D Ⓓ Abiah Ⓒ Doma Group

5A Ⓓ Unibrand Belgrade Ⓒ Iskra   5B Ⓓ Gesture Studio Ⓒ Kay Lab / The University of Utah   5C Ⓓ Martin Jordan Ⓒ Airport Region   5D Ⓓ BrandBerry Ⓒ Valera Namazov

	A	B	C	D

 africa's **THIRST**	 C H R O M A VOCAL ENSEMBLE	 FREEZE	 *downtown* **KC**	**1**
 SIGNAL PATTERNS	 AUSTIN TATIOUS BLINDS AND SHUTTERS	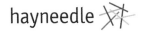 hayneedle		**2**
 Bürgerheim Rheinfelden Gemeinsam leben	 HSBCdirect	 EVENTS FORUM® GLOBAL MEETING & EVENT MANAGEMENT	 PHOENIX park	**3**
 International Festival of Cultural Diversity	 STIKK	 COMUNGU	 CircusOpera	**4**
 *adimurti* ADIMURTI.COM	 CONE SUL	milk factory		**5**

ⓓ = Design Firm   ⓒ = Client

1A ⓓ Stebbings Partners ⓒ Africaâ (tm)s Thirst   1B ⓓ The Creative Method ⓒ Chroma Vocal Ensemble   1C ⓓ creative space ⓒ International Gallery of Contemporary Art   1D ⓓ Blacktop Creative ⓒ The Downtown Council of Kansas City

2A ⓓ Jenny Ng ⓒ Signal Patterns   2B ⓓ fugasi creative ⓒ austintatious Blinds and Shutters   2C ⓓ Lippincott ⓒ Netshop   2D ⓓ KITA International | Visual Playground ⓒ KITA

3A ⓓ Kommunikation & Design ⓒ Bürgerheim Rheinfelden   3B ⓓ Studio Grafik ⓒ Landor Associates   3C ⓓ Draward ⓒ Aleksandrs Kirhensteins   3D ⓓ Hand dizajn studio ⓒ Phoenix Capitis

4A ⓓ Karl Design Vienna ⓒ Unesco (proposal)   4B ⓓ ProjectGraphics ⓒ STIKK   4C ⓓ Logoholik ⓒ Bojan Stefanovic   4D ⓓ Brandmor ⓒ Mako Lehel Mor

5A ⓓ Sergey Shapiro ⓒ Adimurti.com   5B ⓓ Sebastiany Branding & Design ⓒ Cone Sul   5C ⓓ mlQelangelo ⓒ Miroslav Vujovic   5D ⓓ Higher ⓒ Ebooks Corporation

	A	B	C	D
1		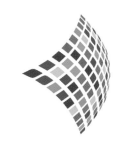		
2				
3				
4				
5				

Ⓓ = Design Firm   Ⓒ = Client

1A Ⓓ Niedermeier Design Ⓒ demandflex   1B Ⓓ Logo Design Works Ⓒ Blue Ram Digital Media   1C Ⓓ Firefly Graphic Design Ⓒ Chris Wiggins   1D Ⓓ Ewert Design Ⓒ Richwine Environmental

2A Ⓓ Kuznetsov Evgeniy | KUZNETS Ⓒ Moscow airline   2B Ⓓ Version-X Design Ⓒ Advertising Rating Company   2C Ⓓ Type G Ⓒ Councel Direct Law Offices   2D Ⓓ dache Ⓒ David Pache

3A Ⓓ Higher Ⓒ Avorio Media   3B Ⓓ EIGHTDAY STUDIO Ⓒ Consultant1   3C Ⓓ Kristian Andersen + Associates Ⓒ Alerding Castor LLP   3D Ⓓ Hand dizajn studio Ⓒ Agitrade

4A Ⓓ Denis Olenik Design Studio Ⓒ Avivo   4B Ⓓ supersoon good design Ⓒ Swiss Heat Transfer Technology   4C Ⓓ T&E Polydorou Design Ltd Ⓒ Trident Developments   4D Ⓓ Eggra Ⓒ Teleco

5A Ⓓ Brandmor Ⓒ Tuly P   5B Ⓓ TypeOrange Ⓒ Available   5C Ⓓ Delevante Ⓒ Anthem Healthcare   5D Ⓓ Ishan Khosla Design Ⓒ Institute for Inner Studies Publishing

A	**B**	**C**	**D**	
 GEE'S BEND QUILTS	 THE GALLERY	 Moda *Modern Living*	 TM	1
 PETERSON'S	 CRESO	 DigiSign	 Briteclick™	2
	 PHOENIX PLAZA	 PHOENIX PENTOMINIUM	 PROTEUS	3
 BAUER DRUCK			 Synfusion	4
 TM	 CARAT Investment Leasing Company	 NAVILLUS		5

Ⓓ = Design Firm   Ⓒ = Client

1A Ⓓ JG Creative Ⓒ Boise Art Museum 1B Ⓓ Mattson Creative Ⓒ p11 Creative 1C Ⓓ Onoma, LLC Ⓒ The Dermot Company 1D Ⓓ Tom Hughes Ⓒ Idealab

2A Ⓓ nelnet Ⓒ Peterson's 2B Ⓓ ARTENTIKO Ⓒ CRESO 2C Ⓓ Gobranding.eu Ⓒ Digi Sign 2D Ⓓ bartodell.com Ⓒ Briteclick.com

3A Ⓓ Kuznetsov Evgeniy | KUZNETS Ⓒ Moscow airline 3B Ⓓ Hand dizajn studio Ⓒ Phoenix Capitis 3C Ⓓ Hand dizajn studio Ⓒ Phoenix Capitis 3D Ⓓ Iconologic Ⓒ Proteus

4A Ⓓ Karl Design Vienna Ⓒ Bauer Druck (proposal) 4B Ⓓ Yotam Hadar Ⓒ Yotam Hadar 4C Ⓓ Anthony Lane Studios Ⓒ Anthony Lane 4D Ⓓ Red Thinking Ⓒ Synfusion

5A Ⓓ bartodell.com Ⓒ Skyfiber (R) 5B Ⓓ Extrabrand Ⓒ Carat Investment 5C Ⓓ Marketsplash by HP Ⓒ Navillus 5D Ⓓ TOKY Branding+Design Ⓒ Brochsteins Woodworking

Austin City Homes
Identity Design

Decoder Ring, Austin, Texas

The new Austin City Homes logo

The progression of trial designs created by Ben Barry and Paul Fucik that led them to the final Austin City Homes logo

Home builder Dan Fawcett didn't have just any dream. He left a major housing company in Austin, Texas, to start his own building company, Austin City Homes. He wanted to create upscale, meticulously crafted, Eichler-inspired houses, and his attention to detail was evident. The first home he built impressed designer Ben Barry.

"The walls are double-thick, and there are floor-to-ceiling windows, custom-built cabinets, two outdoor showers, an outdoor fireplace, five bedrooms, plus a full guest house," explains Barry, one of the designers who helped create the new company's logo. Even the underside of the windowsills got attention. "There is a little cut below each sill so that the water would drip off there, not run down the side of the house."

Every detail had to count to be in keeping with Eichler's modern aesthetic—elegant and spare, yet functional. The same would need to hold true for the design of the new company's logo. At the time, Barry was working as a designer at Decoder Ring (Austin). He and fellow designer Paul Fucik considered what the client asked for in his new identity—something with the same mid-century, modern aesthetic as the architecture, and something that had the same long design legs—something that would remain fresh despite its historical cache.

"This is definitely the kind of design that I love. It's simple and stylish," says Barry, who is now a designer at Facebook. "I like design that does more with less. Paul and I drew in pencil for a while, then onscreen, starting with monograms and letters. Mostly our ideas were purely geometric. When we started drawing the shapes of houses with angular roofs, it started to make sense to turn that into the shape of the letter A."

For the final design, he pulled the black, orange, and green color palette from the house itself, which in turn was borrowed from an original Eichler home.

"We showed it to the client, and he was sold. He loved how it worked," the designer says.

The design team was able to fit the client's brochure, a postcard, and four different business cards on a single, three-color press sheet, so the job was very economical to produce.

"The logo was just one of those where you knew that this was it as soon as we saw it," he adds.

LOGO SEARCH

Keywords  **Symbols**

Type: ◯ Symbol   ◯ Typographic   ◯ Combo   ⬤ All

1

HIMNESKT

no love

gooDEvil

2

green stitch

Handmade
with love

3

LOVE YOUR TEETH

Brosko
для женщин

Lutheran Community Care

4

ANTIOCH
COMMUNITY CHURCH
NORMAN

lutheran
malaria
initiative

Tapestry
CHURCH

5

ⅅ = Design Firm   Ⓒ = Client

1C ⅅ hatchmarks Ⓒ pianolove.org   1D ⅅ McGuire Design Ⓒ Love Bites

2A ⅅ O! Ⓒ Himneskt   2B ⅅ julian peck Ⓒ Julian Peck   2C ⅅ RED The Agency Ⓒ goodEvil Skateboarding   2D ⅅ Gobranding.eu Ⓒ The City of Katowice

3A ⅅ Almosh82 Ⓒ almosh82   3B ⅅ Shark! Ⓒ Gateways School   3C ⅅ artproba creative solutions asia Ⓒ Handmade With Love   3D ⅅ Marketsplash by HP Ⓒ Organic Earth Aid

4A ⅅ T&E Polydorou Design Ltd Ⓒ Kalia Tsangari   4B ⅅ Cheltsov Ⓒ Brosko   4C ⅅ Felixsockwell.com Ⓒ time   4D ⅅ Jolt Ⓒ Lutheran Community Care

5A ⅅ EIGHTDAY STUDIO Ⓒ Antioch Community Church Norman   5B ⅅ Fixation Marketing Ⓒ Lutheran World Relief   5C ⅅ Glitschka Studios Ⓒ Tapestry Church   5D ⅅ LogoDesignGuru.com Ⓒ Christ Clothing

	A	B	C	D
1				
2				
3				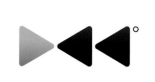
4				
5				

Ⓓ = Design Firm ⒸClient

1A Ⓓ Flaxenfield, Inc. Ⓒ Acceent Urgent Care 1B Ⓓ Rob & Damia Design Ⓒ Communicate Health 1C Ⓓ Just Creative Design Ⓒ Mindful Construct 1D Ⓓ ZORRAQUINO Ⓒ Farmacia Mota Campos

2A Ⓓ PUSH Branding and Design Ⓒ Joppa Outreach Ministries 2B Ⓓ Miriello Grafico, Inc. Ⓒ Yoga Fusion 2C Ⓓ The Office of Art+Logik Ⓒ Dr. Mark Adickes 2D Ⓓ Taylor Design Works Ⓒ Desiring God

3A Ⓓ The Martin Group Ⓒ Renovation Church 3B Ⓓ Muamer Adilovic DESIGN Ⓒ Muamer Adilovic 3C Ⓓ Bronson Ma Creative Ⓒ Fain Models 3D Ⓓ Jan Vranovsky Ⓒ DC Grounds

4A Ⓓ Karl Design Vienna Ⓒ Lujong Eva Furrer 4B Ⓓ Gardner Design Ⓒ Phoenix Productions 4C Ⓓ henriquez lara Ⓒ oligas 4D Ⓓ Stebbings Partners Ⓒ Media Lantern

5A Ⓓ Version-X Design Ⓒ DaBecca Natural Foods 5B Ⓓ Pat Walsh Design, LLC Ⓒ College Fitness 5C Ⓓ Landor Associates Ⓒ UNCF 5D Ⓓ Gardner Design Ⓒ Phoenix Productions

	A	B	C	D

1

2

3

4

5

🅓 = Design Firm   🅒 = Client

1A 🅓 Josh Wallace Graphics and Illustration 🅒 Jim Severson   1B 🅓 City On Fire 🅒 City On Fire   1C 🅓 Ulyanov Denis 🅒 Jinn TV   1D 🅓 Iconologic 🅒 America's Natural Gas Alliance

2A 🅓 Stiles Design 🅒 Sherry Matthews Advocacy Agency   2B 🅓 McGuire Design 🅒 Lone Star Law   2C 🅓 Deney 🅒 Med Construction   2D 🅓 Gardner Design 🅒 Trails Crossing

3A 🅓 McCraw Design 🅒 Texas Land Conservancy   3B 🅓 Pure Fusion Media 🅒 Hollywood Studios Intl   3C 🅓 Rise Design Branding Inc. 🅒 Star Creative   3D 🅓 Kommunikat 🅒 Autentika

4A 🅓 Noble 🅒 American Theatre Company (proposed)   4B 🅓 McGuire Design 🅒 Upstage Talent Recruiters   4C 🅓 Burocratik - Design 🅒 PINHOS   4D 🅓 Michael Nagy 🅒 Europe Entertainment Ltd.

5A 🅓 Balcom Agency 🅒 Justin Boots   5B 🅓 Pure Fusion Media 🅒 Paradis Caviar   5C 🅓 onetreeink 🅒 Fallen Star inc.   5D 🅓 ChapmanCreative 🅒 Texas Hope Literacy

	A	B	C	D
1				
2				
3				
4				
5				

ⓓ = Design Firm   ⓒ = Client

1A ⓓ KROG, d.o.o. ⓒ Veda   1B ⓓ Higher ⓒ Ebooks Corporation   1C ⓓ Siah Design ⓒ Mostly English   1D ⓓ KROG, d.o.o. ⓒ Youth Publishing

2A ⓓ 3x4 Design Studio ⓒ Damoon Publication   2B ⓓ Ulyanov Denis ⓒ LogoBook   2C ⓓ Fernandez Design ⓒ Champion Technologies   2D ⓓ wray ward ⓒ Carolina Pad & Paper

3A ⓓ Lienhart Design ⓒ Springboard Motivation   3B ⓓ Down With Design ⓒ Godiva Books   3C ⓓ Anagraphic ⓒ Luther Publishing Ltd   3D ⓓ Sebastiany Branding & Design ⓒ Santa Marcelina

4A ⓓ Alan Barnet Design ⓒ Orthodox Union Learn   4B ⓓ Gerren Lamson ⓒ A Community For Education (ACE)   4C ⓓ Paul Jobson ⓒ Recycle Bottles   4D ⓓ mlQelangelo ⓒ Miroslav Vujovic

5A ⓓ CAI Communications ⓒ Employer Associations of America   5B ⓓ Chris Rooney Illustration/Design ⓒ Ramsell   5C ⓓ mlQelangelo ⓒ Web Africa (South African ISP)   5D ⓓ Felixsockwell.com ⓒ World AIDS

A Wisp of Tea
Identity Design

Lin Shaobin Design Co., Ltd., Guangdong Province, China

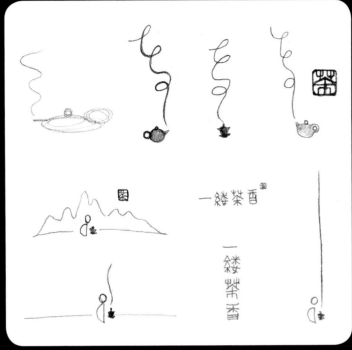

A Wisp of Tea is a very Zen-based tea shop in Guangdong Province, China. Its space could be described as very simple and laconic, a place of peace and thoughtfulness where one can gain refreshment for the body and mind.

The tea served in the shop is from the surrounding mountains. It is unique, made from wild plants that have not been contaminated or treated in any way. The tea is rare and very special, and the shop's owner wanted to convey that in his new identity.

Designer Lin Shaobin, of Lin Shaobin Design Co., Ltd., says the client wanted to express the quality of the shop's products so that they would be enticed to enter the shop by not only his offerings, but also the spirit behind them.

"He wanted to catch the sense of the inspiration, to express the headspring of the shop's feeling in the design," Lin Shaobin explains. "I wanted to bring the imaginary space to the people."

The solution they developed is extraordinarily simple in its rendering but replete with meaning. The barest representation of a person sits in peace, contemplating the small container of brewing tea. The steam from the brew moves slowly heavenward, which could represent inspiration, prayer, or just simple thinking.

"The graphical representation for the words 'a wisp of tea' can be profound as a symbol, so the logo is unique and exquisite. The randomness and abstraction of the design gives space and imagination to the people, with a deep Zen consciousness. So, the logo truly demonstrates the tea's flavor, how to achieve the state of Zen through tea, and to understand the peace, reverence, and simplicity of the spirit of the tea ceremony," Lin Shaobin says.

Above: Designer Lin Shaobin's trials for client A Wisp of Tea centered around the concept of steam. Sketches from the project show how the designer refined the design down to its barest essentials.

LOGO SEARCH

Keywords: **Arts**

Type: ○ Symbol ○ Typographic ○ Combo ● All

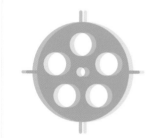

Ⓓ = Design Firm   Ⓒ = Client

1C Ⓓ Dickerson Ⓒ Marcus Dickerson   1D Ⓓ J Fletcher Design Ⓒ Greenlitscripts

2A Ⓓ GeniusLogo Ⓒ africanfilmclub.com   2B Ⓓ PUSH Branding and Design Ⓒ Rogue Media   2C Ⓓ Fangman Design Ⓒ AIGA Austin   2D Ⓓ R&R Partners Ⓒ Airwave

3A Ⓓ McGuire Design Ⓒ Flicks and Food   3B Ⓓ Brent Couchman Design Ⓒ Sniper Twins   3C Ⓓ Porkka & Kuutsa Oy Ⓒ Finnish Floorball Association   3D Ⓓ Siah Design Ⓒ Horror Films

4A Ⓓ oneal design Ⓒ Hot Shots   4B Ⓓ Marlin Ⓒ Click Photography   4C Ⓓ FUEL Creative Group Ⓒ Tracy Birdsell Photography   4D Ⓓ Bridges Design Group Ⓒ Payton Bridges

5A Ⓓ Karl Design Vienna Ⓒ Bodalgo GmbH   5B Ⓓ www.n1kk3l.com Ⓒ Attack Concerts   5C Ⓓ Gearbox Ⓒ Lonely Grange Recorders   5D Ⓓ Device Ⓒ Device

	A	B	C	D	
1					
2					
3					

Ⓓ = Design Firm   Ⓒ = Client

1A Ⓓ BBM&D Strategic Branding Ⓒ Iconix 1B Ⓓ STUBBORN SIDEBURN Ⓒ Vera project 1C Ⓓ Newhouse Design Ⓒ Permanent Record 1D Ⓓ www.MikeyBurton.com Ⓒ MUSIC SAVES Independent Record Store

2A Ⓓ Kuznetsov Evgeniy | KUZNETS Ⓒ sanofi aventis 2B Ⓓ Art Brown Design Ⓒ Milligan College Strings Camp 2C Ⓓ DeShetler Design Ⓒ Haymaker 2D Ⓓ Kaiser Creative Ⓒ Red Hot Group

3A Ⓓ Kuznetsov Evgeniy | KUZNETS Ⓒ sound republic 3B Ⓓ Logoguppy Ⓒ jazzcuzzi 3C Ⓓ ChapmanCreative Ⓒ Van Cliburn Foundation 3D Ⓓ Kevin Zwirble Design Co. Ⓒ Music & Arts Centers

4A Ⓓ D&i (Design and Image) Ⓒ Ben Gust 4B Ⓓ Kevin Zwirble Design Co. Ⓒ Rooftop Communications 4C Ⓓ Almosh82 Ⓒ Almosh82 4D Ⓓ Deep See Design Ⓒ Peter Jones

5A Ⓓ Wizemark Ⓒ 365 Logo Project 5B Ⓓ jo Ⓒ Christine Herbeck 5C Ⓓ RedBrand Ⓒ Barber's shop 5D Ⓓ Hai Truong Ⓒ GoGo Hairdressing

A **B** **C** **D**

1

2

3

4

5

Ⓓ = Design Firm Ⓒ = Client

1A Ⓓ Device Ⓒ Device 1B Ⓓ Nicole Ziegler Ⓒ Jones 1C Ⓓ Meir Billet Ltd. Ⓒ Colors Etc. 1D Ⓓ Stitch Design Co. Ⓒ Marie Lorentz & Turner Watson

2A Ⓓ united* Ⓒ scott conant 2B Ⓓ Barcellona, Inc. Ⓒ Art Foundry & Gallery 2C Ⓓ Luxecetera, Inc. Ⓒ Ashley Jankowski 2D Ⓓ Z&G Ⓒ Alexandr Kalganov

3A Ⓓ Siah Design Ⓒ Josephine Publishing 3B Ⓓ Wizemark Ⓒ 365 Logo Project 3C Ⓓ Rick Johnson & Company, Inc. Ⓒ New Mexico Architecture 3D Ⓓ LONI DBS Ⓒ Book publishers

4A Ⓓ Squid Ink Creative Ⓒ In Stitches 4B Ⓓ Ullman Design Ⓒ Brooklyn Style Foundation; for WÃ(c)yo.org 4C Ⓓ Studio Ink Ⓒ Inspired Needleworks 4D Ⓓ Tran Creative Ⓒ ComfySofas.com

5A Ⓓ Tran Creative Ⓒ RelaxingAdirondackChairs.com 5B Ⓓ Walsh Branding Ⓒ SR Hughes 5C Ⓓ BrandExtract Ⓒ Staged to Sell 5D Ⓓ Schwartzrock Graphic Arts Ⓒ Design Center

LOGO SEARCH

Keywords **Miscellaneous**

Type: ○ Symbol ○ Typographic ○ Combo ● All

A Broken Umbrella Theatre

1

SUCCESS IN THE CITY

32nd Annual Santa Monica Venice Christmas Run December 12 2009

the Bag Lady project

BKSF

2

paper dress studio

BRas ACROSS tHE BRIDGE

3

COLLEGE SAVINGS

KING ☗ BEAN

COFFEE ROASTERS
CHARLESTON, SOUTH CAROLINA

4

PAP ERG UN!

BACKFIRE

SILENCING IS NOT A CRIME

SOCIALBOMB

5

ⓓ = Design Firm ⓒ = Client

1A ⓓ Wizemark ⓒ Srdjan Kirtic 1C ⓓ Vaxa Creative ⓒ Kristen Yngve 1D ⓓ Hole in the Roof ⓒ Brandon HEath

2A ⓓ Red Thinking ⓒ Success in the City 2B ⓓ Ph.D ⓒ Christmas Run 2C ⓓ Pool ⓒ The Bag Lady Project 2D ⓓ Ullman Design ⓒ Brooklyn Style Foundation

3A ⓓ The Pink Pear Design Company ⓒ Kimberly Keller 3B ⓓ Bozell ⓒ Alegent Health 3C ⓓ Deney ⓒ Go4 3D ⓓ brandclay ⓒ Unused

4A ⓓ Matador Design Studio ⓒ United Supermarkets 4B ⓓ Siah Design ⓒ BicycleTutor.com 4C ⓓ Stitch Design Co. ⓒ Kurt Weinberger 4D ⓓ Rovillo Design Associates ⓒ King Cotton

5A ⓓ Just Creative Design ⓒ PaperGun 5B ⓓ Double A Creative ⓒ Backfire 5C ⓓ ten:pm media ⓒ Advanced Armament Corp. 5D ⓓ Sosebee Design ⓒ Socialbomb

	A	B	C	D
1		 IDEALABS		
2	 STATE VOICES			
3	 greenacres			 FOOD WORLD
4	 FULL TIME employment agency	GET ORGANIZED	ticketfeed	
5	 CUSTOM FIT BOOKKEEPING & TAX	 THE GFT	 digbox	 Pride Trade

Ⓓ = Design Firm　Ⓒ = Client

1A Ⓓ Wizemark　1B Ⓓ Dalius Stuoka Ⓒ Idealabs　1C Ⓓ Siah Design Ⓒ Smart Plumbing　1D Ⓓ SOULSEVEN Ⓒ FAME

2A Ⓓ Kristin Spix Design Ⓒ State Voices　2B Ⓓ Glitschka Studios Ⓒ InContext　2C Ⓓ BrandBerry Ⓒ Bidzy　2D Ⓓ Stebbings Partners Ⓒ Rhode Runner

3A Ⓓ mlsane industries Ⓒ Green Acres LLC　3B Ⓓ Torch Creative Ⓒ Mike Thurman　3C Ⓓ Siah Design Ⓒ BuyItSellIt.com　3D Ⓓ elbow Ⓒ Palladeo

4A Ⓓ Dalius Stuoka Ⓒ Dalius Stuoka　4B Ⓓ Wizemark Ⓒ 365 Logo Project　4C Ⓓ dache Ⓒ David Pache　4D Ⓓ O Positive Design, Inc Ⓒ Boy Scouts of America

5A Ⓓ Juicebox Designs Ⓒ Custom Fit Bookkeeping & Tax　5B Ⓓ R&R Partners Ⓒ Randy Heil　5C Ⓓ 01d Ⓒ digbox.ru　5D Ⓓ Sakideamsheni Ⓒ Pride Trade

Dooo Design Studio
Identity Design

Dooo Design Studio, Beijing, China

Dooo Design Studio is a graphic design studio formed by Wenjie Huo (also known as Ksama) and Fengkun Bai, both of whom received master's degrees in art and design from BIFT (Beijing Institute of Fashion Technology). After graduation in 2009, they formed Dooo Design Studio and have gone on to specialize in posters and brand identities.

Faced with the challenge of creating an identity for their own studio, Ksama and his fellow designers wanted to communicate their high standards for design work through their own logo.

"In general, logos should be easily readable, but as the logo of a studio that creates logos, it should be more creative. We want it to be special, not so easy to understand at first glance, but not easy to forget when you get it," says Ksama.

The Dooo Design Studio designers feel that they can always meet clients' needs. But they have an even higher requirement in their own work. Ksama says they strive to be more innovative in their work than what might otherwise be found in their region.

Fonts in China are a good example, says Ksama. Most of the fonts there are very similar, just standard computer faces. So,

when a client might need a unique font for a logo, other designers instead choose to create a unique graphic and mix it with a regular font. Dooo wanted a unique font and graphic for its logo.

The solution that the designers finally developed is based on a Chinese character that has the English pronunciation "doo."

"The right side of the Dooo logo surely looks like a figure of a person. On the left side of it is a simulation of a ruler or scale," explains Ksama. "In Chinese, the character we used means 'measure.' We believe there is a limited zone between good design and bad design."

His team's goal is to make the most outstanding design, so the figure's "arm" is placed high on the scale. The designers chose red for the little person to convey their enthusiasm and energy for the life of design. The result is a design that is readable by Chinese viewers but which can also be read by non-Chinese audiences.

Above: The right side of the Dooo Design logo looks like a person, the left side like a ruler. Actually, the two sides form a Chinese character that has the pronunciation "doo." In Chinese, the word means "measure."

LOGO SEARCH

Keywords: **Food**

Type: ◯ Symbol ◯ Typographic ◯ Combo ⦿ All

art café
GALLERY

The GUTTER
A PLACE IN-BETWEEN.

INTER WINES

FISHBAR

AIGA MINNESOTA

VINO
TÉQUE

MARQUE   DÉPOSÉE
LETOURMENT VERT
ABSINTHE FRANCAISE

GHOST
BAR

LIQUOR
.com

wine
camp BLOG

DRINK
THINK

Ⓓ = Design Firm   Ⓒ = Client

1C Ⓓ Karl Design Vienna Ⓒ Sprachschule Wien   1D Ⓓ RED The Agency Ⓒ guiltlesscafe.com

2A Ⓓ 3x4 Design Studio Ⓒ Music Cafe   2B Ⓓ akapustin Ⓒ Alexander Kapustin   2C Ⓓ AT PACE Ⓒ Arts café   2D Ⓓ Brent Couchman Design Ⓒ Stella

3A Ⓓ Clive Jacobson Design Ⓒ Clive Jacobson Design   3B Ⓓ 3 Advertising LLC Ⓒ The Gutter   3C Ⓓ Strange Ideas Ⓒ James Strange   3D Ⓓ Asgard Ⓒ Fishbar. Wine Restaurant

4A Ⓓ Schwartzrock Graphic Arts Ⓒ AIGA Minnesota   4B Ⓓ Evenson Design Group Ⓒ Vinoteque   4C Ⓓ John deWolf Ⓒ deWolf Beverage Consulting   4D Ⓓ Turner Duckworth Ⓒ Distillerie Vinet EGE

5A Ⓓ Dotzero Design Ⓒ Falcon Art Community   5B Ⓓ R&R Partners Ⓒ Liquor.com   5C Ⓓ Sonia Jones Design Ⓒ Craig Camp   5D Ⓓ Dotzero Design Ⓒ Drink Think

A   **B**   **C**   **D**

     **1**

     **2**

      **3**

      **4**

      **5**

Ⓓ = Design Firm   Ⓒ = Client

1A Ⓓ Yuka Highbridge Ⓒ Bryan Vaniman   1B Ⓓ Down With Design Ⓒ Leisure   1C Ⓓ Michael Spitz Ⓒ Michael Spitz   1D Ⓓ Gramma Ⓒ Vinital

2A Ⓓ Studiofluid Ⓒ Tom Schleuning   2B Ⓓ Iconologic Ⓒ The Coca-Cola Company   2C Ⓓ Turner Duckworth Ⓒ Joshua Michels   2D Ⓓ Naughtyfish Ⓒ Naughtyfish

3A Ⓓ Logorado Ⓒ Nadir Balcikli   3B Ⓓ Gearbox Ⓒ Odell Brewing   3C Ⓓ Strange Ideas Ⓒ James Strange   3D Ⓓ Westwerk DSGN Ⓒ Catlick Records

4A Ⓓ Torch Creative Ⓒ DASA   4B Ⓓ Brandmor Ⓒ Castle Catering   4C Ⓓ Hole in the Roof Ⓒ Spoons   4D Ⓓ Z&G Ⓒ Alexandr Kalganov

5A Ⓓ IF marketing & advertising Ⓒ groovy spoon   5B Ⓓ The O Group Ⓒ Nu-Kitchen   5C Ⓓ Luke Despatie & The Design Firm Ⓒ The Northside   5D Ⓓ Luke Despatie & The Design Firm Ⓒ The Northside

	A	B	C	D
1				
2				
3				
4				
5				CHILUP

Ⓓ = Design Firm   Ⓒ = Client

1A Ⓓ Michael Spitz Ⓒ Michael Spitz   1B Ⓓ Sean Heisler Ⓒ Sean Heisler   1C Ⓓ R&R Partners Ⓒ Airwave   1D Ⓓ Lemon Design Pvt Ltd Ⓒ Cinemon Studios

2A Ⓓ Paul Jobson Ⓒ Delicious Real Estate   2B Ⓓ Michael Spitz Ⓒ Michael Spitz   2C Ⓓ Tarsha Rockowitz Design Ⓒ Cake Fashion Boutique   2D Ⓓ ThreeHouse Design Studio Ⓒ Cups Organic Cupcakes

3A Ⓓ Gyula Nemeth Ⓒ Ab Ovo Studio   3B Ⓓ Luke Despatie & The Design Firm Ⓒ Wishbone   3C Ⓓ Propaganda Inc. Ⓒ Metromedia Restaurant Group   3D Ⓓ Design Hub Ⓒ Downtown Hays Development Corp.

4A Ⓓ Steve Biel Design Ⓒ Savitski Design/A Different Dog   4B Ⓓ Propaganda Inc. Ⓒ Metromedia Restaurant Group   4C Ⓓ noe design Ⓒ Sakari Sushi Lounge   4D Ⓓ Adept Interactive Ⓒ Water-asian food bar

5A Ⓓ Banowetz + Company, Inc. Ⓒ Kent Rathbun   5B Ⓓ Just Creative Design Ⓒ Thaiphoon   5C Ⓓ Anna Kovecses Ⓒ taco mortale   5D Ⓓ Logoholik Ⓒ Bojan Stefanovic

	A	B	C	D

    1

    2

    3

    4

    5

Ⓓ = Design Firm   Ⓒ = Client

1A Ⓓ lunabrand design group Ⓒ The Peanut Shell   1B Ⓓ Turner Duckworth Ⓒ Christian Eager   1C Ⓓ H2 Design of Texas Ⓒ Alexis Moreno   1D Ⓓ Boswell Design Solutions Ⓒ Wolfgang Puck

2A Ⓓ Siah Design Ⓒ freshfruitbaskets.com   2B Ⓓ Trilix Ⓒ Tangerine Food Company   2C Ⓓ Studio2 Ⓒ Orange Julius of America   2D Ⓓ Evenson Design Group Ⓒ Blake Brand Growers

3A Ⓓ Nynas Ⓒ Thinking Out of a Box   3B Ⓓ studio sudar d.o.o. Ⓒ Balenovic   3C Ⓓ Aron Creative Ⓒ Applebees   3D Ⓓ Almosh82 Ⓒ slicedlemon films

4A Ⓓ Iconologic Ⓒ MS&L Worldwide   4B Ⓓ Nectar Graphics Ⓒ Baird Family Orchards   4C Ⓓ R&R Partners Ⓒ Airwave   4D Ⓓ Extrabrand Ⓒ Adv Gudzon

5A Ⓓ Entermotion Design Studio Ⓒ Green Pantry   5B Ⓓ Doink, Inc. Ⓒ South Beach Food and Wine Festival   5C Ⓓ United by Design Ⓒ Victoria Stewart & Flavia Rose   5D Ⓓ Troyca - Visual Solutions GmbH Ⓒ Hochschule RheinMain

LOGO SEARCH

Keywords **Structures**

Type: ○ Symbol ○ Typographic ○ Combo ● All

Ⓓ = Design Firm   Ⓒ = Client

1C Ⓓ Kristin Spix Design Ⓒ Kristin Spix   1D Ⓓ Koetter Design Ⓒ Foundation for the Homeless

2A Ⓓ Studio International Ⓒ Our Home   2B Ⓓ Andrei Bilan Ⓒ Pro Casa   2C Ⓓ JRDG Brand Design & Communications Ⓒ Jewish Recovery Houses   2D Ⓓ Bridges Design Group Ⓒ Home Business Connection

3A Ⓓ Dalius Stuoka Ⓒ Houseclip Housing   3B Ⓓ julian peck Ⓒ openhouse.com   3C Ⓓ Strange Ideas Ⓒ James Strange   3D Ⓓ Mattson Creative Ⓒ Pocono Modern

4A Ⓓ Device Ⓒ Maria Cabardo   4B Ⓓ Alphabet Arm Design Ⓒ Placetailor   4C Ⓓ Version-X Design Ⓒ GrooveHouse   4D Ⓓ Mattson Creative Ⓒ Pocono Modern

5A Ⓓ Schwartzrock Graphic Arts Ⓒ Enhanced Landscaping   5B Ⓓ Yury Akulin | Logodiver Ⓒ My House   5C Ⓓ Mattson Creative Ⓒ Pocono Modern   5D Ⓓ Kuznetsov Evgeniy | KUZNETS Ⓒ Region Sistem

1

2

3

4

5

ⓓ = Design Firm   ⓒ = Client

1A ⓓ Ishan Khosla Design ⓒ Random House India   1B ⓓ Bozell ⓒ TownCommons.com   1C ⓓ Jill McCoy Design ⓒ Mimi Braatz/Braddock & Logan   1D ⓓ Brand Innovation Group ⓒ The RedBarn Market.com

2A ⓓ Retro DC ⓒ Gadget Factory   2B ⓓ Freshwater Design ⓒ KnockKnock Industries   2C ⓓ The Infantree ⓒ The Factory Youth Center   2D ⓓ Gizwiz Studio ⓒ ReciproCity

3A ⓓ Asgard ⓒ Baltika Business Centre   3B ⓓ Strange Ideas ⓒ James Strange   3C ⓓ Bailey Lauerman ⓒ James Strange   3D ⓓ Asgard ⓒ Podvorie Russian Restaurant

4A ⓓ Kendall Creative Shop, Inc. ⓒ LNR   4B ⓓ RARE Design ⓒ The Depot Coffee House and Sweet Shop   4C ⓓ Evoke International Design ⓒ Boutique Empire   4D ⓓ Device ⓒ Device

5A ⓓ Banowetz + Company, Inc. ⓒ Law Office of Joseph E. Ashmore   5B ⓓ Winking Fish ⓒ East Akron Neighborhood Development Corporation (EANDC)   5C ⓓ grow ⓒ Museum of Islamic Arts   5D ⓓ Device ⓒ Rian Hughes

	A	B	C	D
1				
2				
3				
4				
5				

Ⓓ = Design Firm   Ⓒ = Client

1A Ⓓ Paspartu Ⓒ Sacvoyage   1B Ⓓ agregidea Ⓒ Mercado Global   1C Ⓓ Michael Spitz Ⓒ Michael Spitz   1D Ⓓ Logorado Ⓒ Eskeemo

2A Ⓓ Koodoz Design Ⓒ Bridge Road Early Learning Centre   2B Ⓓ Neworld Associates Ⓒ Irish Rural Tourism Federation   2C Ⓓ Rose Ⓒ Belron International   2D Ⓓ Kastelov Ⓒ Michael Bridges

3A Ⓓ visuALchemy Ⓒ Bridges Pub & Eatery   3B Ⓓ Jeremy Honea Ⓒ Aquarelle   3C Ⓓ Wizemark Ⓒ 365 Logo Project   3D Ⓓ Visual Language LLC Ⓒ The Garden Club of Irvington-on-Hudson

4A Ⓓ JM Design Co. Ⓒ Fox Theater   4B Ⓓ Limon Agencia Creativa Ⓒ Municipio de Hopelchén   4C Ⓓ feltinc.com Ⓒ The State of Florida   4D Ⓓ The Greater Good Design Ⓒ Project Offland

5A Ⓓ ginger griffin marketing and design Ⓒ Dora Blaskievich   5B Ⓓ Siah Design Ⓒ Office Strategies   5C Ⓓ Filip Komorowski Ⓒ Krzysztof Łada   5D Ⓓ Stephens Studio Ⓒ French American International School

LOGO SEARCH

A   **B**   **C**   **D**

Keywords  **Transportation**

○ Symbol   ○ Typographic   ○ Combo   ● All

1

2

3

4

5

🄳 = Design Firm   🄲 = Client

1C 🄳 Mikolaj Humienny 🄲 Express   1D 🄳 X3 Studios 🄲 City Cars

2A 🄳 01d 🄲 MyCarwash   2B 🄳 Bailey Lauerman 🄲 James Strange   2C 🄳 Tactix Creative 🄲 Paul Howalt   2D 🄳 The Netmen Corp 🄲 HRCA

3A 🄳 Level B Design 🄲 Bryan Sanford   3B 🄳 Storm Design Inc. 🄲 Factory 1969   3C 🄳 Gyula Nemeth 🄲 Tiny Red Bus   3D 🄳 Hole in the Roof 🄲 Red Truck Renovations

4A 🄳 Equity Brand Design 🄲 Ozark Overall Company   4B 🄳 Home Grown Logos 🄲 Otto & Sons Nursery   4C 🄳 01d 🄲 BigAll   4D 🄳 PaperSky Design 🄲 Walt's Coffee

5A 🄳 Studio No. 6 🄲 Pedal To Properties   5B 🄳 NOT A CANNED HAM 🄲 REI   5C 🄳 Duffy & Partners 🄲 City of Minneapolis   5D 🄳 The Joe Bosack Graphic Design Co. 🄲 Carew Co.

	A	B	C	D
1	 **RED BIKE** JUICE BAR & BISTRO	 pedalpushers	 RE:CREATION	 Lee Jackson
2		Scoot	 vivavivir pre · post · natal	 CRIPPLED BY SPECIAL INTERESTS
3			 THE FARM	 RED TRACTOR Farm
4	 HARVEST FARE	 TRACTOR®	 REEL FARM	 ФОРЕНТ
5	 OCTA	 REDCABOOSE HOBBY STORE		 MAKE UP NOT WAR

Ⓓ = Design Firm   Ⓒ = Client

1A Ⓓ Green Ink Studio Ⓒ Green Ink Studio 1B Ⓓ Connie Aridas Creative Ⓒ Connie Aridas 1C Ⓓ NoCo Ⓒ recreation studio 1D Ⓓ Roy Smith Design Ⓒ Carl Durban/Lee Jackson

2A Ⓓ Fifth Letter Ⓒ Camel City Cruisers 2B Ⓓ Rick Johnson & Company, Inc. Ⓒ ABQ Scoot 2C Ⓓ LOWE-SSP3 S.A. Ⓒ Viva Vivir 2D Ⓓ Steven O'Connor Ⓒ Steven O'Connor

3A Ⓓ Chris Rooney Illustration/Design Ⓒ The Little Red Wagon Daycare 3B Ⓓ Yury Akulin | Logodiver Ⓒ Railway Portal 3C Ⓓ Riley Designs Ⓒ The Farm 3D Ⓓ Amanda Warren :: design :: illustration :: books Ⓒ Jess Pierson

4A Ⓓ Neworld Associates Ⓒ Boyne Valley Foods 4B Ⓓ Naughtyfish Ⓒ Tractor design School 4C Ⓓ Michael Spitz Ⓒ Michael Spitz 4D Ⓓ Extrabrand Ⓒ Forent Technica

5A Ⓓ Fusion Advertising Ⓒ Oak Cliff Transit Authority 5B Ⓓ Genaro Solis Ⓒ Red Caboose (unused) 5C Ⓓ R&R Partners Ⓒ Western High Speed Rail Alliance 5D Ⓓ Karl Design Vienna Ⓒ Karl Design Vienna

A	B	C	D	
				1
				2
				3
				4
				5

ⓓ = Design Firm   ⓒ = Client

1A ⓓ Fargo Design Co., Inc. ⓒ Trip Witt Travel   1B ⓓ Alphabet Arm Design ⓒ Elly Hartshorn & Josh McFadden   1C ⓓ Michael Spitz ⓒ Michael Spitz   1D ⓓ Roy Smith Design ⓒ Advanta/The Point

2A ⓓ Sean Heisler ⓒ Sean Heisler   2B ⓓ Pure Fusion Media ⓒ Aeromax Balloon Productions   2C ⓓ EIGHTDAY STUDIO ⓒ Metro Point Lending   2D ⓓ Strange Ideas ⓒ James Strange

3A ⓓ Kuznetsov Evgeniy | KUZNETS ⓒ Moscow airline   3B ⓓ Logoholik ⓒ skyoflove.org   3C ⓓ Caliber Creative, LLC ⓒ Caliber Creative   3D ⓓ Michael Spitz ⓒ Michael Spitz

4A ⓓ Sabingrafik, Inc. ⓒ Sage Harbor—Ira Investments   4B ⓓ 2TREES DESIGN ⓒ Garganos   4C ⓓ Sabingrafik, Inc. ⓒ Possible Dreams   4D ⓓ Kommunikat ⓒ Jakub Rutkowski

5A ⓓ 01d ⓒ Charter Club   5B ⓓ Marketsplash by HP ⓒ Blue Canoe   5C ⓓ Koetter Design ⓒ Proposed to the City of Louisville   5D ⓓ Gesture Studio ⓒ Oneironautics

index

You can access a fully searchable database of logos featured in this and all other LogoLounge books by purchasing a membership to www.logolounge.com. With your membership, you can search for logos by keyword, client or design firm name, client industry, or type of mark, and get designer credits and contact information for each logo as well. The database is always growing: In fact, your membership also allows you to upload an unlimited number of your own logos, each of which will be considered by our judges for inclusion in upcoming LogoLounge books.

directory

01d
Belarus
+375 29 6601228
www.01d.ru

1981
USA
404-368-5770
www.nineteeneightyone.com

28 LIMITED BRAND
Germany
+49234-91 60 95-1
www.twenty-eight.de

2TREES DESIGN
USA
515-314-9934
www.2treesdesignco.com

3 Advertising LLC
USA
505-293-2333
www.whois3.com

3906 Design
USA
910-620-2542
www.3906design.com

3x4 Design Studio
Iran

484 Design, Inc.
USA
315-534-0067

5Seven
USA
415-385-4521
www.fivesevendesign.com

903 Creative, LLC
USA
434-774-5164
www.903creative.com

a. pounds design
USA
214-491-9177

A.D. Creative Group
USA
406-248-7117
www.adcreativegroup.com

A3 Design
USA
585-542-8303
www.athreedesign.com

Aars | Wells
USA
214-446-0996

ab designwerks
USA
817-991-5280
www.abdesignwerks.com

Abiah
USA
609-653-2233
www.abiah.com

Able
USA
757-672-6921
www.designedbyable.com

The Action Designer
Norway
0047 47 02 64 01
www.actiondesigner.com

adamgf
UK
7792935377
www.adamgf.com

ADC Global Creativity
USA
214-526-1420
www.adc-inc.com

Adept Interactive
Bulgaria
+359 2 987 6761
www.adeptplayground.com

agregidea
USA
210-860-9404
www.agregidea.com

AHEAD
USA
508-985-9898
www.aheadweb.com

akapustin
Russia
+7 9167538141
www.akapustin.ru

AkarStudios
USA
310-393-0625
www.akarstudios.com

AkinsParker Creative
USA
949-724-8000
www.akinsparker.com

Alan Barnet Design
USA
212-675-0041
www.alanbarnett.com

alekchmura.com
Poland
+48 0 792 370 107
www.alekchmura.com

Alik Yakubovich agency
Russia
8 831 430 15 41
www.newyour.ru

Allison Emery Creative
USA
254-624-1472
www.ajecreative.com

Almosh82
India
www.almosh82.com

Alphabet Arm Design
USA
617-451-9990
www.alphabetarm.com

Altagraf
USA
267-342-3815

Amanda Warren :: design :: illustration :: books
USA
785-760-4429

American Coatings Association
USA
202-719-3694
www.paint.org

Anagraphic
Hungary
+36 1 202 0555
www.anagraphic.hu

Andrea Nassar
Lebanon
961 [03] 249973
www.andreanassar.net

Andrei Bilan
Romania
40742147660

Andrei D. Popa
Romania
40743121822
www.andreipopa.ro

Anna Kövecses
Hungary
003620 4288714
www.annakovecses.com

Anthony Lane Studios
USA
763-245-8243
www.012485.com

Archrival
USA
402-435-2525
www.archrival.com

ARGUS
USA
415-247-2800

Arispe Creative
USA
210-355-3619

Armada d. o. o.
Slovenia
00 386 40 609901

Aron Creative
USA
770-714-6420
www.aroncreative.com

Aroosha Design
USA
408-910-0430

Art Brown Design
USA
423-384-1997
www.artbrowndesign.com

Art Machine
Germany
+49 030 31 50 56 66
www.julianhrankov.com

ARTENTIKO
Poland
793338001
www.artentiko.com

Artini Bar Designs
USA
949-874-5393
www.artinibar.com

Artisticodopeo Designz
India
9325633698
www.artisticodopeo.com

artproba creative solutions asia
Thailand
66894085921

artslinger
Canada
780-884-2242
www.artslinger.ca

Asgard
Russia
79219322216
www.asgard-design.com

AT PACE
South Africa
216745990

Aurum Design
USA
414-777-0015
www.aurum-design.com

Axygene
Canada
514-677-6587

Bailey Lauerman
USA
402-479-0235

Balcom Agency
USA
817-877-9933
www.balcomagency.com

ballard::creative
USA
817-917-6086
www.ballardcreative.com

Banowetz + Company, Inc.
USA
214-823-7300 ext. 100
www.banowetz.com

Barcellona, Inc.
USA
916-642-2484
www.designfelt.com

Barral
France
+33 (0)6 26 11 07 82
www.fabienbarral.com

bartodell.com
USA
806-392-6446
www.bartodell.com

Bauerhaus Design, Inc.
USA
314-398-5790

BBDO Branding
Russia
+7 495 787 57 78
www.bbdo-branding.ru

BBM&D Strategic Branding
USA
805-667-6671

Benedict Sato Design
Australia
03 9809 0484
www.benedictsato.com

Bernas Design
USA
858-775-0855
www.bernasdesign.com

Bertz Design Group
USA
860-347-4332
www.bertzdesign.com

Betterweather
USA
303-956-6946

Black Bridge
USA
303-304-9395

blacksheepdesign
New Zealand
+64 6 353 1983
www.blacksheepdesign.co.nz

Blacktop Creative
USA
816-221-1585
www.blacktopcreative.com

Blue Clover
USA
210-223-5409
www.blueclover.com

Blue Tricycle, Inc.
USA
612-790-7365
www.bluetricycle.com

BluesCue Designs
Philippines
639166079550
www.bluescue.com

Boswell Design Solutions
USA
702-606-1227

Boxon Vision
Bahrain
+973 36760101

Bozell
USA
402-965-4300
www.bozell.com

Brand Agent
USA
214-979-2047

Brand Harvest Consultancy Pvt Ltd
India
+91 09323174028

The Brand Hatchery
USA
214-252-1690

Brand Innovation Group
USA
260-469-4060

BrandBerry
Russia
89171091522
www.brand-berry.ru

brandclay
USA
734-260-9771
www.brandclay.com

BrandExtract
USA
713-942-7959

The Brandit
USA
910-508-9938

BrandLab Moscow
Russia
+7 (495) 775-1280
www.brandlab.ru

Brandmor
Romania
40723450094
www.brandmor.ro

brandStrata
USA
562-594-6761
www.brandstrata.com

BrandWell Creative
USA
650-871-1611

Braue: Brand Design Experts
Germany
+49.471.983820
www.braue.info

Brent Couchman Design
USA
214-755-0368
www.brentcouchman.com

Brian Haselton
USA
704-763-2499
www.brianhaselton.com

Bridges Design Group
USA
512-557-2966
www.bridgesdesigngroup.com

Britt Funderburk
USA
917-721-8382
www.brittfunderburk.com

Bronson Ma Creative
USA
214-457-5615
www.bronsonma.com

Brotbeck Corporate Design AG
Switzerland
41323451481

BRUEDESIGN
USA
952-200-9279
www.nickbrue.com

Bryan Cooper Design
USA
918-605-1084
www.cooperillustration.com

Burocratik—Design
Portugal
351239499110
www.burocratik.com

C7 Design
New Zealand
+64 6 769 6482
www.cseven.co.nz

CAI Communications
USA
919-878-9222
www.caicommunications.com

Caliber Creative, LLC
USA
214-741-4488
www.calibercreative.com

Caliente Creative
USA
512-627-2607
www.calientecreative.com

Campbell Fisher Design
USA
602-955-2707
www.thinkcfd.com

Canyon Creative
USA
702-262-9901
www.canyoncreative.com

Carrihan Creative Group
USA
214-658-1588
www.carrihan.com

Carve
Canada
519-663-5996
www.carvedesign.ca

Caspari McCormick
USA
302-421-9080
www.casparimccormick.com

Cassie Klingler Design
USA
435-757-7852
www.cassieklingler.com

catherine blomkamp
South Africa
27834476848

Ceb Design
Canada
416-226-9761
www.cebdesign.com

Cerny Product Development, Inc.
USA
650-326-2711
www.cernypd.com

CF Napa Brand Design
USA
707-265-1891
www.cfnapa.com

Chad Mjos
USA
918-813-1922

Chameleon Design Group, LLC
USA
508-439-4800
www.chameleondg.com

ChapmanCreative
USA
214-902-8471
www.chapmancreative.us

Cheltsov
Russia
79104751528
www.cheltsov.com

Chen Design Associates
USA
415-896-5338
www.chendesign.com

Chris Herron Design
USA
773-278-8070
www.chrisherrondesign.com

Chris Rooney Illustration/Design
USA
415-827-3729
www.looneyrooney.com

Chris Trivizas | Design
Greece
302109310803
www.christrivizas.eu

Christopher Dina
USA
646-489-5246
www.christopherdina.com

Christopher Labno
Poland
501639902
www.crislabno.com

CINDERBLOC CREATIVE
Canada
416-777-2562
www.cinderbloc.com

Citizen Studio
USA
404-892-0560
www.citizenstudio.com

City On Fire
USA
415-350-6870
www.cityonfire.us

Clashmore
USA
757-817-2052

Clay McIntosh Creative
USA
918-591-3070
www.claymcintosh.com

Clive Jacobson Design
USA
212-912-9139
www.clivejacobson.com

Clockwork Studios
USA
210-545-3415 ext. 107

Colin Saito
USA
562-682-4292
www.colinsaito.com

Combustion
USA
901-544-9500
www.thesparkmachine.com

Communication Agency
Slovakia
421907915937
www.communicationagency.com

concussion, llc
USA
817-336-6824 ext. 207

Connie Aridas Creative
USA
828-232-7222

Cooper Design
USA
512-762-2623

Cooper Smith and Company
USA
515-244-4133

CopperCoast
South Africa
27117834527
www.coppercoast.co.za

Creative Beard
USA
949-413-3774
www.creativebeard.com

The Creative Method
Australia
+61 2 8231 9977

creative space
USA
907-632-5782

The Creative System
USA
804-888-6380
www.thecreativesystem.com

Cricket Design Works
USA
608-255-0002
www.cricketdesignworks.com

Croak Design
UK
7732873982
www.croakdesign.co.uk

crookedjaw design
USA
414-559-8943

Cubic
USA
918-587-7888
www.cubiccreative.com

Cuie&Co
South Africa
27214619031
www.cuieandco.com

cultiva
USA
740-837-6085

Culture Pilot
USA
713-868-4100

D&Dre Design
USA
512-577-9189
www.deandredesign.com

D&i (Design and Image)
USA
303-292-3455
www.seebrandgo.com

D*MN Good
USA
202-288-3390

dache
Switzerland
+41 78 683 37 59
www.dache.ch

dale harris
Australia
411899840
www.daleharris.com

Dalius Stuoka
Lithuania
37067275323
www.behance.net/houston_we

Dallas Duncan Design
USA
404-374-6539
www.dallasduncan.com

Daniel Fernandez
USA
407-221-5542
www.dffernandez.com

Dara Creative
Ireland
00 353 1 672 5222
www.daracreative.ie

Darling Design
USA
212-929-8480

David Clark Design
USA
918-295-0044
www.davidclarkdesign.com

David Gramblin
USA
918-261-2042

Davina Chatkeon Design
USA
818-953-7143
www.davinachatkeon.com

dbDESIGNS
Germany
496082924548
www.dbdesigns.de

dee duncan
USA
316-204-3873
www.deeduncan.com

Deep See Design
USA
480-703-7367

DEI Creative
USA
206-281-4004

Deksia
USA
515-720-0227
www.deksia.com

Delevante
USA
615-383-4700
www.delevantecreative.com

Deney
Turkey
902164287997
www.deney.com.tr

Denis Olenik Design Studio
Belarus
+37529 7580457
www.denisolenik.com

Depikt
USA
305-975-5169
www.depikt.com

Derrick Mitchell Design, LLC
USA
509-953-3364
www.mitchell07.com

DeShetler Design
USA
206-434-1931
www.deshetlerdesign.com

Design & Co
USA
617-524-1856

Design Army
USA
202-797-1018
www.designarmy.com

The Design Engine, LLC
USA
414-587-2827
www.thedesignengine.com

Design Hub
USA
785-434-2777
www.dessinfournir.com

Design Invasion
USA
314-226-1694

Design Practice, Inc.
USA
714-832-3520

DesignPoint, Inc.
USA
503-364-2970
www.designpointinc.com

designproject
USA
312-379-8656
www.designprojectweb.com

designsgirl
USA
303-453-9235

Dessein
Australia
61.8.9228.0661
www.dessein.com.au

Deutsch Design Works
USA
415-487-8520

DEVELOPED IMAGE PTE LTD
Singapore
6597862302

Device
UK
347-535-0626 (USA)
www.devicefonts.co.uk

dialog
USA
201-432-2765

Diana Graham
Germany
-102233

Diann Cage Design
USA
314-503-4001
www.dianncage.com

Dickerson
USA
817-207-9009

diffuse.ru
Russia
79265295542
www.diffuse.ru

DikranianDesign
USA
203-767-3964

Distillery Design Studio
USA
608-255-0092

Diva Design
USA
212-633-2828
www.divadesign.com

DL Designs
USA
206-313-2591

DNKSTUDIO
Ukraine
+38 067 966 3496

Doink, Inc.
USA
305-529-0121
www.doinkdesign.com

Donnie Martello
USA
407-375-9702

Dotzero Design
USA
503-892-9262
www.dotzerodesign.com

Double A Creative
USA
402-719-5362
www.doubleacreative.com

Double O Design
Ireland
00353 17642001
www.doubleodesign.com

Douglas Beatty
UK
+44 079 603 007 12

Down With Design
UK
+447595369273

Dragon Lunchbox
USA
254-744-7872

Draward
Latvia
37126834475
www.draward.com

The Drawing Board
USA
352-346-8948
www.tdbgraphics.com

Dreambox Creative
USA
916-705-0406
www.dreamboxcreative.com

Drink Red Creative
USA
323-965-1948

d-signbureau
Germany
815195468

DTM_INC
The Netherlands
075 635 52 46

Du4 Designs
USA
619-342-6488
www.du4designs.com

Duffy & Partners
USA
612-548-2333
www.duffy.com

DUSTIN PARKER ARTS
USA
316-993-1397
www.dustinparkerarts.com

Eben Design
USA
206-523-9010
www.ebendesign.com

Effusion Creative Solutions
USA
480-227-8951
www.effusiondesign.com

Eggra
Macedonia
38970390144
www.eggra.com

Ehlinger
USA
832-444-8020

eight a.m. brand design (shanghai) Co., Ltd
China
8621 64583036
www.8-a-m.com

EIGHTDAY STUDIO
USA
405-315-8880
www.eightdaystudio.com

Eiland Design
USA
334-821-9576

El Paso, Galeria de Comunicacion
Spain
+34 91 594 22 48
www.elpasocomunicacion.com

elbow
USA
415-738-8833
www.elbow.com

Elements
USA
203-776-1323

Elevation Creative Studios
USA
www.elevationcreative.com

eleven07
USA
347-683-8414

Emilio Correa
Mexico
+52 55 5712 7910
www.emiliographics.com

Empax
USA
212-242-5300
www.empax.org

Entermotion Design Studio
USA
316-264-2277
www.entermotion.com

entz creative
Singapore
62554353
www.entzcreative.com

Equity Brand Design
USA
262-764-5520

Essex Two
USA
773-489-1400
www.sx2.com

Evenson Design Group
USA
310-204-1995
www.evensondesign.com

Evoke International Design
Canada
605-875-8667
www.evoke.ca

Ewert Design
USA
503-692-5513
www.ewertdesign.com

EXPLORARE
Mexico
52 (222) 230-4152
www.explorare.com

Extrabrand
Russia
+7 926 837-67-95
www.extrabrand.ru

Extralarge, A Design Studio
USA
760-683-4911
www.xlstudios.com

Factor Tres
Mexico
(+5255)55688335
www.factortres.com.mx

Fangman Design
USA
512-426-3252
www.fangmandesign.com

Fargo Design Co., Inc.
USA
412-311-6100
www.fargodesignco.com

Farm Design
USA
310-461-4054
www.farmdesign.net

Felixsockwell.com
USA
917-657-8880
www.felixsockwell.com

feltinc.com
USA
727-512-5717
www.feltinc.com

Fernandez Design
USA
512-619-4020
www.fernandezdesign.com

Ferreira Design Company
USA
678-297-1903

Fezlab
USA
520-514-7024
www.fezlab.com

Fierce Competitors
USA
203-506-0030

Fifth Letter
USA
336-723-5655
www.fifth-letter.com

Filip Komorowski
Poland
600337232
www.behance.net/komorowski

Firefly Branding Boutique
Romania
40722426522
www.firefly.ro

Firefly Graphic Design
USA
317-985-2781
www.fireflycarmel.com

Fitch Seattle
USA
206-624-0551
www.fitch.com

Fixation Marketing
USA
240-207-2009
www.fixation.com

Flash Bang
USA
512-637-8999

Flaxenfield, Inc.
USA
919-644-6444
www.flaxenfield.com

Fleishman Hillard
USA
314-982-9149

Flight Deck Creative
USA
214-534-9468
www.flightdeckcreative.com

Floc5
USA
913-636-2614
www.floc5.com

Floris Design
The Netherlands
628512012
www.florisdesign.com

Flying Hand Media
USA
216-906-6219

For the Love of Creating
USA
770-516-7301
www.fortheloveofcreating.com

FORM
USA
216-921-9460

Franke+Fiorella
USA
612-338-1700
www.frankefiorella.com

Freight Train
USA
414-226-2113
www.freighttraincreative.com

Fresh Creative
Indonesia
(+6221)5210851
www.freshandcreative.com

Freshwater Design
USA
601-835-8569
www.rhondafreshwater.com

FUEL Creative Group
USA
916-669-1591

fugasi creative
USA
512-576-5460
www.fugasicreative.com

Fuller
Australia
+61 8 8363 6811
www.fuller.com.au

Fumiko Noon
USA
619-261-7118
www.fumikodesign.com

Fusion Advertising
USA
214-453-4545

Galperin Design, Inc.
USA
212-873-1121
www.galperindesign.com

Gardner Design
USA
316-691-8808
www.gardnerdesign.com

Gary Sample Design
USA
513-271-7785

Gavula Design Associates
USA
917-863-8076
www.gavuladesign.com

Gearbox
USA
541-549-1478

Genaro Solis
USA
210-508-0225

GeniusLogo
Serbia
+381 64 2 655433
www.geniuslogo.com

Gerren Lamson
USA
210-854-8699
www.gerrenlamson.com

Gesture Studio
USA
801-419-0993
www.gesturestudio.com

Ghiath Lahham
UAE
971507829509
www.ghiathlahham.com

Gibson
UK
020 8948 9656
www.thisisgibson.com

ginger griffin marketing and design
USA
704-896-2479
www.wehaveideas.com

GingerBee Creative
USA
406-443-3032

Gizwiz Studio
Malaysia
604 228 9931
www.logodesigncreation.com

Glacier
USA
801-369-3130
www.glaciermark.com

Glitschka Studios
USA
971-223-6143
www.glitschka.com

Go Welsh
USA
717-898-9000
www.gowelsh.com

Gobranding.eu
Poland
48.507123635
www.gobranding.eu

Gramma
Belgium
3232609907
www.gramma.be

Graphic design studio
by Yurko Gutsulyak
Ukraine
380674465560
www.gstudio.com.ua

Graphismo
USA
512-686-1495
www.graphismo.com

The Greater Good Design
USA
www.greatergooddesign.com

Green Ink Studio
USA
415-203-4164
www.greeninkstudio.com

Greenhouse Studio
USA
904-356-8630
www.gogreenhouse.com

Grindell Design
USA
203-641-5377
www.grindelldesign.com

GripNStay LLC
USA
903-724-2608

Gröters Design
Germany
+49 (0) 8142 6523987
www.groeters.de

grow
Qatar
00974 444 6222
www.growqatar.com

gtc media
USA
305-608-7269

GUIPON M.D.S.
Ecuador
59342837392

Gyula Nemeth
Hungary
36 20 429 2019
www.seadevilworks.blogspot.com

H.
Mexico
(999) 9271122
www.hcreativos.com

H2 Design of Texas
USA
512-775-7350
www.h2dot.com

Hai Truong
Australia
+61 (0) 419 394 575
www.hai.com.au

Hand dizajn studio
Croatia
38512333489
www.hand.hr

hatchmarks
USA

Hayes Image
Australia
52471433
www.hayesimage.com.au

Hazen Creative, Inc.
USA
312-451-5413
www.hazencreative.com

Headwerk
USA
602-952-2530
www.headwerk.com

Heisel Design
USA
941-922-0492
www.heiseldesign.com

Helikopter Reklambyra
Sweden
46911221060
www.helikopter.nu

Helius Creative Advertising
USA
801-673-4199
www.flickr.com/photos/helius_creative/
sets

henriquez lara
Mexico
(52) 33 15 94 73 49
www.henriquezlara.com

Hernandez Design Studio
USA
210-859-8239
www.hernandezdesignstudio.com

Hibblen Design
USA
918-366-2033

Higher
Belarus
375336013875

Hilary Dana Williams
USA
865-591-8595
www.hilarydana.com

Hive Communication
Australia
61266807875

Hole in the Roof
USA
254-756-1200

Holler Design
USA
813-253-2050
www.hollerdesign.com

Home Grown Logos
USA
707-338-1271
www.homegrownlogos.com

HOOK
USA
843-853-5532
www.hookusa.com

Hotbed Creative
USA
317-631-2097
www.hotbedcreative.com

Hubbell Design Works
USA
714-227-3457
www.hubbelldesignworks.com

huebner petersen
USA
970-663-9344
www.huebnerpetersen.com

Hvita husid
Iceland
+354 562 1177

Iconologic
USA
404-260-4500
www.iconologic.com

ID.Brand
Indonesia
6221 5826311
www.idbrand.co.id

idApostle
Canada
www.idapostle.com

IDEGRAFO
Romania
+40 742 959 457
www.idegrafo.com

identity kitchen
USA
818-459-3993

Identity33
USA
260-580-0099
www.identity33.com

IF marketing & advertising
USA
512-930-5558
www.intra-focus.com

Igor Duibanov
Russia
www.russoturisto.deviantart.com

iHook Creative
USA
916-276-0614
www.ihookcreative.com

iHua Design
USA
415-203-9048
www.ihuadesign.com

Imadesign, Corp.
Russia
+7 495 775 4810
www.imadesign.ru

Imagine Creative
Australia
1300 139 398

Incey Wincey
UK
7990574304

Incitrio
USA
858-202-1822

Indaco
Italy
+39 349 7511471
www.studioindaco.eu

Indelible
USA
818-288-2676

Indicia Design Inc
USA
816-471-6200
www.indiciadesign.com

The Infantree
USA
717-394-6932
www.theinfantree.com

Infestation
South Africa
27847525375
www.behance.net/erwinbindeman

insight design
USA
956-580-1544

Insight Marketing Design
USA
605-275-0011
www.insightmarketingdesign.com

interbrand
USA
212-798-7646
www.interbrand.com

Interrobang Design Collaborative, Inc.
USA
802-434-5970
www.interrobangdesign.com

Ishan Khosla Design
India
91-9958333006
www.ishankhosladesign.com

ivan_aran_design_studio
Serbia
38163330629

izm
USA
435-901-1533
www.whalenlouis.com

J Fletcher Design
USA
843-364-1776
www.jfletcherdesign.com

Jackrabbit Design
USA
617-298-6200
www.jumpingjackrabbit.com

The Jake Group, LLC
USA
202-333-2850
www.thejakegroup.com

jamjardesign
Lebanon
+961 3 385885
www.jamjardesign.com

Jan Sabach Design
USA
718-310-8966
www.sabach.cz

Jan Vranovsky
Czech Republic
www.ra30412.com

Jarek Kowalczyk
Poland
+48 502634695
www.jarekkowalczyk.com

Jase Neapolitan Design
USA
301-514-9789

Jason Drumheller
USA
443-742-7375
www.jasondrumheller.com

Jason Kirshenblatt
USA
212-327-0777

Jedzkolor
Poland
795599010
www.jedzkolor.com

Jeff Kern Design
USA
417-234-4709
www.723design.com

Jeffhalmos
Canada
416-850-9616
www.jeffhalmos.com

Jenny Ng
USA
646-283-6878
www.jennyng.com

Jeremy Honea
USA
405-315-4764

Jeremy Slagle Design
USA
614-804-6234

Jerron Ames
USA
801-636-7929

Jesse Kirsch
USA
917-331-6837
www.jessekirsch.com

JG Creative
USA
208-440-2301
www.jgc.me

Jill McCoy Design
USA
408-267-4652

JM Design Co.
USA
831-771-9831
www.jmdesignco.net

JM Designs
USA
970-290-7061
www.jm-designs.com

jo
USA
718-496-5983
www.jofolio.com

Joan Pons Moll
Spain

The Joe Bosack Graphic Design Co.
USA
215-766-1461
www.joebosack.com

John deWolf
USA
202-657-7111

Johnston Duffy
USA
215-389-2888
www.johnstonduffy.com

Jolt
Australia
+61 7 3216 0656
www.joltstudio.com.au

Jon Briggs Design
USA
760-707-6453
www.creativehotlist.com/jbriggs2

Jon Kay Design
USA
352-870-8438
www.jonkaydesign.com

jonskaggs.com
USA
847-877-4002

Josef Stapel
Germany
496190931907
www.josefstapel.de

Josh Berta
USA
646-981-3023

josh higgins design
USA
619-379-2090
www.joshhiggins.com

Josh Wallace Graphics
and Illustration
USA
651-278-3740
www.joshwallace.com

JRDG Brand Design &
Communications
USA
203-256-0934
www.jrdg.com

Juan Pablo Tredicce
Argentina
(+54 11) 3808 9988

Juancazu
Colombia
3188134249

Judson Design
USA
713-520-1096
www.judsondesign.com

Juggler Design
Australia
+61 3 9444 0623
www.juggler.com.au

Juicebox Designs
USA
615-297-1682

julian peck
USA
415-246-4897

Just Creative Design
Australia
+61 411 402 312
www.justcreativedesign.com

Kaiser Creative
USA
818-755-5045

KarbonBlack Creative
South Africa
826154978

Karl Design Vienna
Austria
0043-1-208 66 53
www.karl-design-logos.com

Kastelov
Bulgaria
359886034151
www.kastelov.com

keith cummings
USA
814-355-1964

Kelley Nixon
USA
512-878-1182

Kendall Creative Shop, Inc.
USA
214-827-6680

KENNETH DISENO
Mexico
(52) 452 523 1738
www.kengraf.net

Keo Pierron
USA
515-203-9430

Kessler Design Group
USA
301-907-3233

Kevin Zwirble Design Co.
USA
781-572-7876
www.coroflot.com/kzwirble

The Key
Australia
+61 423 011 409
www.whproject.com

Kilmer & Kilmer
USA
505-260-1175
www.kilmer2.com

Kindred Design Studio, Inc.
USA
802-482-5535
www.kindredesign.com

KITA International | Visual Playground
Germany
+49.30.54714690
www.kita-berlin.com

Klik-Dizajn
Poland
48501149883
www.klik-dizajn.pl

Klundt Hosmer
USA
509-456-5576
www.klundthosmer.com

Koetter Design
USA
502-515-3092

Kolar Advertising and Marketing
USA
512-345-6658

Kommunikat
Poland
+48 506275302
www.kommunikat.pl

Kommunikation & Design
Germany
497751897400
www.kommunikation-design.de

kommunikativ
Germany
492521821261

KONIAK DESIGN
Israel
972547866026
www.behance.net/gorzio

KONZEPT DESIGN ILLU
Germany
0049-163-4049490

Koodoz Design
Australia
61 3 9568 5559
www.koodoz.com.au

Kreativer Kopf
Germany
491773292728

Kristian Andersen + Associates
USA
317-713-7500
www.kristianandersen.com

Kristin Spix Design
USA
917-521-0484
www.kristinspixdesign.com

KROG, d.o.o.
Slovenia
+386 41 780 880
www.krog.si

Kuznetsov Evgeniy | KUZNETS
Russia
79101517929
www.kuznets.net

KW43 BRANDDESIGN
Germany
+ 49 211 557783-10
www.kw43.de

Label Brand
USA
614-291-4534
www.labelbrand.com

Landkamer Partners, Inc.
USA
415-239-2680
www.landkamerpartners.com

Landor Associates
USA
212-614-5261
www.sfo.landor.com

Latinbrand
Ecuador
593 2 2461075
www.latin-brand.com

laurendesigns
USA
585-507-6923
www.laurendesigns.com

LeBoYe
Indonesia
62 21 7199676
www.leboyedesign.com

Lemon Design Pvt Ltd
India
912064782278
www.lemondesign.co.in

Letter+Five
USA
651-983-5193

Level B Design
USA
515-669-8418
www.levelbdesign.com

Lienhart Design
USA
312-399-8047
www.lienhartdesign.com

Limelight Advertising & Design
Canada
905-885-9895
www.limelight.org

Limon Agencia Creativa
Mexico
9811441558

LindyLazar Marketing
USA
231-932-1526
www.lindylazar.com

Lippincott
USA
212-521-0010
www.lippincott.com

lis design
USA
518-306-4198
www.lisdesign.com

Little Box Of Ideas
Australia
61424962505

THE LIVING CONSPIRACY
Germany
497146283725
www.the-living-conspiracy.net

LOCHS
The Netherlands
31235299299
www.lochs.nl

Logo Design Works
USA
216-373-0612
www.logodesignworks.com

LogoDesignGuru.com
USA
877-525-5646
www.logodesignguru.com

Logoguppy
India
919686862297

Logoholik
Serbia
914 595 6926
www.logoholik.com

Logorado
Turkey
905427186318
www.logorado.com

LONI DBS
Slovenia
38631419688

Love Communications
USA
801-364-6865
www.lovecomm.net

LOWE-SSP3 S.A.
Colombia
57 1 6058000

Lucero Design
USA

Luke Baker
USA
801-471-3559
www.lucasmarc.com

Luke Despatie & The Design Firm
Canada
416-995-0243
www.thedesignfirm.ca

lunabrand design group
USA
480-429-3774
www.lunabrands.com

Lunar Cow
USA
800-594-9620
www.lunarcow.com

Luxecetera, Inc.
USA
800-607-0991

M. Brady Clark Design
USA
512-698-9025
www.mbradyclark.com

mlsane industries
USA
617-577-6468
www.msaneindustries.com

M10 Design
Brazil
+55.61.3967.0619
www.m10.com.br

M3 Advertising Design
USA
702-460-1904
www.m3ad.com

mabu
Denmark
+0045 25872363
www.mabu.dk

Mahimoto
Canada
416-975-0084
mahimoto.com

Majorminor
USA
415-504-3462
www.majorminorsf.com

Make Area
Russia
+7 906 728 40 47

Manifest Communications
Canada
416-593-7017 ext. 256

maria guarracino
USA
614-284-9997

markatos | moore
USA
415-235-9203
www.mm-sf.com

Marketsplash by HP
USA
801-692-2576
www.marketsplash.com

markosoti.com
USA
847-744-0144
www.markosoti.com

Marlin
USA
417-885-4530
www.marlinco.com

The Martin Group
USA
716-853-2757
www.martingroupmarketing.com

Martin Jordan
Germany
-5035435
www.martinjordan.de

Mary Hutchison Design LLC
USA
206-407-3460
www.maryhutchisondesign.com

Matador Design Studio
USA
806-553-5489
www.matadordesignstudio.com

Matchstic
USA
404-446-1517
www.matchstic.com

Matthew Wells Design
Canada
778-773-1145
www.matthewwells.ca

Mattson Creative
USA
949-651-8740
www.mattsoncreative.com

max2o
USA
770-454-7100 ext. 107
www.max2oadvertising.com

Maycreate
USA
423-634-0123
www.maycreate.com

McCraw Design
USA
512-301-8772

McGuire Design
USA
210-884-4609
www.mcguiredesign.com

McMillian Design
USA
718-636-2097
www.mcmilliandesign.com

MDM Design
Australia
+613 9639 3399
www.mdmdesign.com.au

Meir Billet Ltd.
Israel
-5626608

Michael Nagy
Austria
436769216812
www.michaelnagy.at

Michael Spitz
USA
267-519-1008
www.michaelspitz.com

Mikolaj Humienny
Poland
-506143088
www.mhumienny.pl

Miles Design
USA
317-915-8693
www.milesdesign.com

Miller Creative LLC
USA
732-905-0844
www.yaelmiller.com

milou
Poland
48664771121
www.themilou.com

Mindgruve
USA
619-757-1325 ext. 231
www.mindgruve.com

MINE
USA
415-647-6463
www.minesf.com

mlQelangelo
Serbia
381641179800
www.miqelangelo.com

Miriello Grafico, Inc.
USA
619-234-1124
www.miriellografico.com

Mission Creative
USA
563-583-0853
www.missioncreative.biz

Mission Minded
USA
415-680-5864
www.mission-minded.com

The Modern Brand Company
USA
205-705-3776
www.themodernbrand.com

Molly McCoy
USA
510-547-8908
www.mollymccoy.com

Mongoose—The Web Company
USA
214-717-5122
www.mongooseco.com

moosylvania
USA
314-644-7900
www.moosylvania.com

More Branding+Communication
USA
918-519-1605

Moss Creative
USA
602-410-3203
www.mosscreative.com

Motto
USA
843-916-0402

MP Design
Poland
48606782797

Muamer Adilovic DESIGN
Bosnia & Herzegovina
38733532126
www.logotip.ba

Muhina Design
Russia
+7(3412) 52-56-71
www.muhinadesign.ru

Murillo Design, Inc.
USA
210-248-9412
www.murillodesign.com

Nadim Twal
Jordan
962777850805
www.nadimtwal.com

Najlon
Croatia
+385 1 4650747
www.najlon.hr

Nastasha Beatty Designs
USA
201-234-7560

The Navicor Group
USA
614-543-6499

Naughtyfish
Australia

Nectar Graphics
USA
503-472-1512
www.nectargraphics.com

nelnet
USA
402-323-4663

The Netmen Corp
Argentina
5411-4776-3684
www.thenetmencorp.com

NewCity
USA
540-552-1320

Newhouse Design
USA
406-600-6532

Neworld Associates
Ireland
+353 1 4165600
www.neworld.com

Nicole Ziegler
USA
717-372-0437
www.nicolezieglerdesign.com

Niedermeier Design
USA
206-351-3927

Ninet6 Ltd
UK
7765670144
www.ninet6.com

Noble
USA
417-875-5000
www.noble.net

NoCo
Serbia
381641473355

noe design
USA
515-597-4286
www.noedesign.com

Noesis
UK
+44 (0)20 7240 1499

NOMADESIGN Inc.
Japan
362773877
www.nomadesign.jp

Nordyke Design
USA
860-233-8874

Noriu Menulio (Current)
Lithuania
37067113180
www.noriumenulio.lt

NOT A CANNED HAM
USA
404-316-2132

Nynas
USA
214-566-5166

The O Group
USA
212-398-0100
www.ogroup.net

O Positive Design, Inc
USA
630-636-9321

O!
Iceland
+354 562 3300
www.oid.is

The Office of Art+Logik
USA
612-599-0286

Oleg Peters
Russia
+7 915 434 07 42
www.yarvu.ru

oLo Brand group
USA
212-529-2861
www.ologroup.com

One up
Romania
004 0722 616 739
www.one-up.ro

oneal design
USA
513-829-1187
www.onealdesigns.com

onetreeink
USA
www.onetreeink.com

Onoma, LLC
USA
212-253-6570
www.onomadesign.com

Orange Label
Czech Republic
+420 775 619 415
www.orangelabel.com

orangebird
USA
614-302-5906

ORFIK DESIGN
Greece
306932909191
www.orfikdesign.gr

origo branding company
USA
614-784-0020
www.origobranding.com

Oxide Design Co.
USA
402-344-0168
www.oxidedesign.com

PaperSky Design
USA
408-340-7902
www.paperskydesign.com

Paradox Box
Russia
79177519251
www.paradoxbox.ru

Paraphernalia Design
Australia
416173462

Partners + Napier
USA
585-454-1010
www.partnersandnapier.com

Paspartu
Russia
79094546468
www.artpaspartu.ru

Pat Walsh Design, LLC
USA
440-995-5118

Patten ID
USA
517-627-2033
www.pattenid.com

Paul Jobson
USA
864-420-8998
www.pauljobson.com

Pavone
USA
717-234-8886

PenPixel Design
USA
631-751-0077
www.penpixeldesign.com

Pentagram Design
USA
512-476-3076

Periscope
USA
612-399-0461

Peter Gale Graphic Design
Australia
61 8 8362 6849

petervasvari.com
Hungary
+36 209 349 873
www.petervasvari.com

Ph.D
USA
310-829-0900
www.phdla.com

Phony Lawn
USA
720-273-1414
www.phonylawn.com

phyx design
USA
562-301-4889

Pierpoint Design + Branding
USA
509-466-1565
www.pierpointwebsite.com

The Pink Pear Design Company
USA
816-519-7327
www.pinkpear.com

Pixelube
USA
206-216-0278
www.pixelube.com

planet of shapes
Mauritius
2307908157

PLAY Creative
USA
402-613-7973
www.playcreativedesign.com

Pointsmith
USA
281-582-1276

POLLARDdesign
USA
503-246-7251
www.pollarddesign.com

Pool
USA
970-247-2262
www.poolcreative.us

Pop Ovidiu Sebastian
Romania
+40.728.297.829
www.brandcore.ro

Porch Creative
USA
601-707-7625

Porkka & Kuutsa Oy
Finland
+358 207401696
www.porkka-kuutsa.fi

pricedyment
Canada
905-309-3701
www.pricedyment.ca

Primarily Rye LLC
USA
615-397-9595
www.primarilyrye.com

ProjectGraphics
Kosovo
37744124139
www.projectgraphics.eu

Propaganda Inc.
USA
314-664-8516

Ptarmak, Inc.
USA
512-772-2852
www.ptarmak.com

Pure Fusion Media
USA
615-329-3235
www.purefusionmedia.com

PurEthanol
USA
832-748-7010

PUSH Branding and Design
USA
515-288-5278
www.pushbranding.com

The Queen City Studio
USA
716-903-2570
www.thequeencitystudio.com

R&R Partners
USA
702-228-0222

Rachel Castor
USA
913-908-6485

RADAR Agency
USA
817-737-3656
www.radaragency.com

rainy day designs
USA
970-963-9748
www.rainydaydesigns.org

rajasandhu.com
Canada
647-501-7252
www.rajasandhu.com

Ramp
USA
213-623-7267
www.rampcreative.com

Range
USA
214-744-0555
www.rangeus.com

RARE Design
USA
601-544-7273
www.raredesign.com

raudesign
USA
206-778-6086

RawType
USA
952-454-3460
www.behance.net/rawtype

Ray Dugas Design
USA
334-844-3384
cadc.auburn.edu/graphicdesign/ray.html

Razor Creative
Canada
506-382-4200
www.razorcreative.com

Red Clover Studio
USA
206-683-2314

RED The Agency
Canada
780-426-3627
www.redtheagency.com

Red Thinking
USA
703-283-4700
www.redthinkingllc.com

RedBrand
Russia
+7(495) 772-39-39
www.golovach.ru/works
www.redbrand.ru/projects/field/catalog3

RedSpark Creative Ltd
New Zealand
93370305
www.redspark.co.nz

Refinery Design Company
USA
563-584-0172

Reghardt
South Africa
+2783 5664688
www.reghardt.com

Retro DC
USA
517-342-1010
www.retrodc.com

RetroMetro Designs
Canada
604-939-9310
www3.telus.net/retrometro

RICH design studio
Kazakhstan
7273836645
www.richdesign.kz

Richard Baird Ltd
UK
7931131587
www.richardbaird.co.uk

Rick Johnson & Company, Inc.
USA
505-266-1100

Rick Landon Design
USA
214-543-0678
www.ricklandondesign.com

Rickabaugh Graphics
USA
614-337-2229
www.rickabaughgraphics.com

Rico Maier Communication Design (B.A)
Switzerland
044 930 56 61
www.ricomaier.ch

Riggs Partners
USA
803-799-5972
www.riggspartners.com

Riley Designs
USA
303-949-0806
www.rileyhutchens.com

Rise Design Branding Inc.
China
86-533-3118581
www.risedesign.cn

Rispler&Rispler Designer Partnerschaftsgesellschaf
Germany
4921133679770

Rizoma Identidad Visual
Ecuador
593 2 2253334
www.rizoma.com.ec

Rob & Damia Design
USA
413-587-9263

Robin Easter Design
USA
865-524-0146

The Robin Shepherd Group
USA
904-359-0981

Rock Creek Strategic Marketing
USA
301-657-0800

Rocket Science
USA
513-398-1700
www.rocketsciencedesign.net

RocketDog Communications
USA
206-254-0248
www.rocketdog.org

Roger Oddone Design Studio
Brazil
+55 11 9598 7198
www.rogeroddone.com.br

Romulo Moya / Trama
Ecuador
593 2 2246315
www.trama.ec

RONODESIGN
Thailand
66 86 9937197
www.ronodesign.blogspot.com

Rose
UK
020 7394 2800
www.rosedesign.co.uk

Roskelly Inc.
USA
401-683-5091
www.roskelly.com

Ross Clodfelter Design
USA
336-403-9396
www.rossclodfelter.com

Rovillo Design Associates
USA
214-526-6132
www.rovillodesign.com

rowland design & art direction
USA
804-301-7651

Roy Smith Design
UK
+44 (0)7767 797525
www.roysmithdesign.com

Rpd Design
Brazil
55 51 33886387

Rudy Hurtado Global Branding
Canada
416-525-2210
www.rudyhurtado.com

Rufuturu
Russia
8 905 250 64 75
www.rufuturu.ru
www.welcomemedia.ru

Rusty George Creative
USA
253-284-2140
www.rustygeorge.com

Ryan Kegley
USA
816-728-5049
www.ryankegley.com

Ryan Miller Design
USA
317-703-8442
www.ryanmillerdesign.com

Ryan Russell Design
USA
814-880-6377

S Design Inc.
USA
405-608-0556
www.sdesigninc.com

Sabin Design
USA
541-915-0776
www.sabindesign.com

Sabingrafik, Inc.
USA
760-431-0439
www.tracysabin.com

Sakideamsheni
Georgia
995 71 992250

Sanders Design
USA
316-618-1821

SANDIA, Inc.
USA
719-473-8900

Sandra Murray Design
USA
415-888-2187
www.workingdesigner.com

Sauvage Design
New Zealand
+64 9 630 6280
www.sauvage.co.nz

Schifino Lee Advertising
USA
813-258-5858
www.schifinolee.com

Schwartzrock Graphic Arts
USA
952-994-7625
www.schwartzrock.com

Scott Oeschger
USA
610-497-1101
www.scottoeschger.com

Sean Heisler
USA
402-917-6100
www.etherealbrands.com

Sebastiany Branding & Design
Brazil
55 11 3926-3937
www.sebastiany.com.br

see+co
Australia
0413 595 575

seekvisum graphics
Russia

SEMAFOR
Poland
+48 602 744 996

Sergey Shapiro
Russia
+7 962 969 2114
www.fromtheska.ru

Seven25 Design & Typography
Canada
604-685-0097

SGNL Studio
USA
405-514-5158
www.thesgnl.com

Shark!
UK
1422375333

Shelby Designs & Illustrates
USA
510-444-0502

Siah Design
Canada
406-290-0088
www.siahdesign.com

SignalSmith Design
South Africa
+27 (0)83 458 6245

Six17
USA
619-778-9893
www.six17.net

Sky High Advertising FZ LLC
UAE
971502823226
www.skyhighadv.net

Skye Design Studios
USA
910-814-7546
www.skyedesignstudios.com

Small Dog Design
Australia
61 3 5333 7777
www.smalldog.com.au

Smith & Jones
USA
518-272-2400
www.smithandjones.com

Sniff Design Studio
USA
866-712-1994
www.sniffdesign.com

Sockeye Creative
USA
503-226-3843
www.sockeyecreative.com

Sol Consultores
Mexico
(011)(525)56586300
www.solconsultores.com.mx

Sommese Design
USA
814-353-1951

Sonia Jones Design
USA
503-577-9501
www.soniajonesdesign.com

Sosebee Design
USA
917-463-4614
www.sosebeedesign.com

SOULSEVEN
USA
612-214-2656
www.soulseven.com

SparrowDesign
Poland
48607910785
www.sparrowdesign.pl

Special Modern Design
USA
323-258-1212
www.specialmoderndesign.com

Splash:Design
Canada
250-868-1059
www.splashdesign.biz

Spoonbend
USA
512-472-3227
www.spoonbend.com

Spring Advertising + Design
Canada
604-683-0167
www.springadvertising.com

Spring Interactive
Hungary
3630855354
www.spring.hu

Squid Ink Creative
USA
316-260-3805
www.squidinkcreative.com

Stebbings Partners
USA
508-699-7899
www.stebbings.com

Stefan Romanu
Romania
0040 356 108 638
www.stefanromanu.com

Stephens Studio
USA
619-246-1932
www.stephens-studio.net

Steve Biel Design
USA
262-439-9423
www.stevebiel.com

Steve Cantrell
USA
954-574-0601

Steve Davis Design
USA
919-839-2140

Steven O'Connor
USA
323-779-5600

Stiles Design
USA
512-633-9247
www.brettstilesdesign.com

Stitch Design Co.
USA
843-722-6296

Stoller Design Group
USA
510-658-9771

Storeyville
USA
919-577-9299

Storm Design Inc.
Canada
403-239-9401
www.stormdesigninc.com

Strange Ideas
USA
402-479-0224
www.baileylauerman.com

Strategy Design
Australia
+61 2 9251 8137

STUBBORN SIDEBURN
USA
206-388-5052
www.stubbornsideburn.com

Studio 2108
USA
314-865-5088
www.studio2108.com

Studio Grafik
Serbia
381638100682
www.grafik.rs

Studio Hill Design
USA
505-242-8300

Studio Ink
Australia
+61 35441 5991

Studio International
Croatia
www.studio-internaional.com

Studio No. 6
USA
303-652-6230
www.studiono6.com

Studio Rayolux
USA
206-353-1385

studio sudar d.o.o.
Croatia
385989836579
www.iknowsudar.com

Studio2
USA
651-768-7222
www.studio2info.com

Studiofluid
USA
323-309-3396
www.studiofluid.com

Stuph Clothing
USA
615-336-4334
www.stuphclothing.com

Sudduth Design Co.
USA
512-632-6150
www.sudduthdesign.com

Sunday Lounge
USA
719-207-4616
www.sundaylounge.com

SUPERRED
Russia
+7 926 213 7070
www.superred.ru

supersoon good design
Germany
+49 40 60 73 32 94
www.supersoon.net

Suprematika
Russia
89263025067
www.suprematika.ru

Sussner Design Company
USA
612-339-2886

Swingset-Imagination
USA
512-417-9092
www.bafriesen.com

Synsation Graphic Design
Australia
+61(0)293652826
www.synsation.com.au

T E D D Y S H I P L E Y
USA
704-649-4659
www.theodoreshipley.com

T&E Polydorou Design Ltd
Cyprus
+357 24654898
www.polydoroudesign.com

Tactical Magic
USA
901-722-3001
www.tacticalmagic.com

Tactix Creative
USA
480-688-8881
www.tactixcreative.com

TAMER KOSELI
Turkey
+90 544 878 33 24
www.tamerkoseli.com

Tannehill Design
USA
916-688-7870

tarsadia hotels
USA
949-610-8042

Tarsha Rockowitz Design
USA
206-437-7327

Taylor Design Works
USA
651-766-1030
www.taylordesignworks.com

Taylor Vanden Hoek
USA
616-745-1650

ten:pm media
USA
571-235-3099

Tetro Design Incorporated
Canada
204-942-0708
www.tetrodesign.com

Theory Associates
USA
415-904-0995
www.theoryassociates.com

Thinking*Room Inc.
Indonesia
628128867800
www.thinkingroominc.com

Third Planet Communications
USA
412-251-5643

Thomas Cook Designs
USA
919-274-1131
www.thomascookdesigns.com

ThreeHouse Design Studio
USA
858-349-0840

Tim Frame Design
USA
614-598-0113
www.timframe.com

Timber Design Company
USA
317-213-8509
www.timberdesignco.com

Today
Belgium
+32 496 08 66 85

Todd Linkner Design Associates
USA
718-207-0682
www.toddlinkner.com

TOKY Branding+Design
USA
314-534-2000
www.toky.com

Tom Hughes
USA
781-504-3229
www.tomhughesdesign.com

Tom Robinson Graphic Design
USA
215-990-0572

Tomasz Politanski Design
Poland
+48 515 23 23 04
www.tomaszpolitanski.com

TOMCOM, Konzeption und Gestaltung
Germany
-6208041
www.tomcom-online.de

TomJon Design Co.
USA
270-746-9928
www.tomjon.net

Tomko Design
USA
602-412-4002
www.tomkodesign.com

Toolbox Creative
USA
970-493-5755
www.toolboxcreative.com

Torch Creative
USA
214-340-3938
www.torchcreative.com

TPG Architecture
USA
212-536-5205
www.tpgarchitecture.com

Traction
USA
513-579-1008
www.teamtraction.com

Traction
USA
517-482-7919
www.projecttraction.com

Tran Creative
USA
208-664-4098
www.tran-creative.com

Transformer Studio
Russia
+7 985 115 40 43
www.transformerstudio.ru

Trapeze
Canada
250-380-0501
www.trapeze.ca

TriLion Studios
USA
785-841-5500
www.trilionstudios.com

Trilix
USA
515-221-4900

TRK Studio
USA
425-591-1128
www.trkstudio.com

Troyca—Visual Solutions GmbH
Germany
0049-69-74223653

TRUF
USA
310-392-3848
www.trufcreative.com

TunnelBravo
USA
480-649-1400

Turner Duckworth
USA
415-675-7777
www.turnerduckworth.com

Turnpost
USA
402-345-5959

Tweet Design
USA
404-441-0337
www.tweetdesign.com

Twhite
USA
954-591-0852
www.twhitedesign.com

Type G
USA
858-792-7333
www.launchtypeg.com

TypeOrange
USA
414-430-7030

Ullman Design
USA
740-373-2400
www.ullmandesign.com

UlrichPinciotti Design Group
USA
419-255-4515
www.updesigngroup.com

Ulyanov Denis
Russia
8 903 659 5304
www.caspa.ru

Unibrand Belgrade
Serbia
38111627652
www.unibrand360.com

United by Design
UK
(0788) 762-4484
www.ubdstudio.co.uk

united*
USA
917-734-7493

University of North Texas
USA
940-231-1884
www.dining.unt.edu

Univisual
Italy
39026684268
www.univisual.com

Unreal
USA
228-424-2779
www.unrealllc.com

Vanessa Adão
USA
310-867-9348
www.vanessa-adao.com

Vaxa Creative
USA
508-243-3794
www.vaxacreative.com

Version-X Design
USA
818-847-2200
www.version-x.com

Victor Goloubinov
Russia
+7(909)635-93-25
www.revision.ru/authors/3187

VINNA KARTIKA design
Indonesia
+6281 129 8445

Visual Language LLC
USA
914-693-7799
www.visuallanguage.net

Visual Unity
Australia
03 95920622
www.visualunity.com.au

visuALchemy
India
+91 98335 75503
www.behance.net/visualchemy
www.coroflot.com/rawheat

Visualism
Germany
+49(0)40696666848
www.visualism.de

VIVA Creative Group
USA
915-543-9445
www.vivacreativegroup.com

Vlad Ermolaev
Russia
+7 916 555 9038

Voicebox Creative
USA
415-674-3204

volatile-graphics
UK
+44 (0)7976691230
www.volatile-graphics.co.uk

Voov Ltd.
Hungary
0036-20/33-94-922
www.voov.hu

W Creative / Brauer Design Co.
USA
612-723-1473
www.wcreative-mpls.com

Walsh Branding
USA
918-743-9600
www.walshbranding.com

Watel Design
USA
773-880-5070
www.wateldesign.com

Webster Design Associates Inc.
USA
402-551-0503
www.websterdesign.com

Westwerk DSGN
USA
612-251-4277
www.westwerkdesign.com

Whaley Design, Ltd
USA
651-645-3463

Wibye Advertising & Graphic Design
UK
44(0)7905378868

wierhouse
USA
706-447-2630
www.wierhouse.com

William Herod Design
USA
206-669-7294
williamheroddesign.com

Winking Fish
USA
703-312-0782

Wizemark
Serbia
381640691393
www.coroflot.com/wizelizard

Worth | Design
USA
602-466-2460

wray ward
USA
704-332-9071
www.wrayward.com

www.macamecanica.com
Portugal
351917408493
www.macamecanica.com

www.MikeyBurton.com
USA
330-704-9667
www.mikeyburton.com

www.n1kk3l.com
Bulgaria
359895755701
www.n1kk3l.com

X3 Studios
Romania
40729154969
www.x3studios.com

XY ARTS
Australia
www.xyarts.com.au

Yatta Yatta Yatta
USA
509-996-2899

Yotam Hadar
Israel
www.yotamhadar.com

Yuka Highbridge
USA
www.yukahighbridge.com

Yury Akulin | Logodiver
Russia
+7 921 957 79 48
www.logodiver.com

Z&G
Russia
73432133345
www.zg-company.ru

Zieldesign
USA
415-282-4040
www.zieldesign.net

Zookeeper
USA
323-652-2887
www.zookeeper.com

ZORRAQUINO
Spain
+34 944157379
www.zorraquino.com

Zync
Canada
416-322-2865
www.zync.ca

about the authors

Bill Gardner is president of Gardner Design in Wichita, Kansas, and has produced work for Cessna, Thermos, Pepsi, Pizza Hut, Kroger, Hallmark, Cargill Corporation, and the 2004 Athens Olympics. His work has been featured in *Communication Arts, Print, Identity, Graphis, New York Art Directors,* the Museum of Modern Art, and many other national and international design exhibitions. He is the founder of LogoLounge.com and the author of *LogoLounge 1, 2, 3, 4,* and *5,* the *LogoLounge Master Library* series, and the annual *LogoLounge Logo Trend Report.*

Catharine Fishel specializes in working with and writing about designers and related industries. Her writing has appeared in many leading publications. She is editor of the website www.Logo Lounge.com, contributing editor to *PRINT,* and the author of many books about design, including all of the LogoLounge and LogoLounge Master Library books, *Inside the Business of Graphic Design, How to Grow as a Graphic Designer, The Freelance Design Handbook,* and *The In-House Design Handbook.*